Culturally Intelligent Leadership

Culturally Intelligent Leadership

Leading Through Intercultural Interactions

Mai Moua

First published in 2010 by
Business Expert Press, LLC
222 East 46th Street, New York, NY 10017
www.businessexpertpress.com

ISBN-13: 978-1-60649-151-5 (paperback)

ISBN-13: 978-1-60649-152-2 (e-book)

DOI 10.4128/ 9781606491522

A publication in the Business Expert Press Human Resource Management and Organizational Behavior collection

Collection ISSN: 1946-5637 (print)
Collection ISSN: 1946-5645 (electronic)

Cover design by Jonathan Pennell
Interior design by Scribe Inc.

First edition: December 2010

10 9 8 7 6 5 4 3 2 1

Printed in the United States of America.

Abstract

Culturally Intelligent Leadership outlines the important concepts of cultural intelligence (CI) and the steps that must be practiced to become a culturally intelligent leader. CI is both a strategy and a tool that leaders can use to gain more confidence and proficiency when working across cultures. This book outlines the importance of understanding culture and its impact on organizations, the strategic value of cultural intelligence, and the significance of integrating and practicing cultural intelligence in everyday business life. When all these aspects are properly integrated and applied in the leadership and management process, organizations are more innovative and adaptable to respond to cultural changes.

Keywords

cultural intelligence, diversity, leadership, culture, inclusion, cultural competence, cultural diversity

Contents

Preface

As a young Hmong American child growing up in two cultures, I played a game where I guessed the cultural background of everyone around me, regardless of their ethnicity or race, gender or class. It was my version of the game "I Spy," a popular game in the United States that encourages children to be observant of, and learn to identify, objects, places, people, and things. My elementary school teacher taught me the game, and because I wanted to be "just like every American child," I played it every time I had the opportunity. At that time, I did not realize that I was categorizing the things "I spied" into boxes:

> I spy a White person who goes to church.
> I spy a rich, White man going to work.
> I spy a Black man running to catch the bus.

I did not know about "labels" and "stereotypes" and how an innocent game of observation can become harmful in creating blind spots, yet be powerful in bringing to the surface one's assumptions and perceptions.

As an educator and consultant, I use this personal story in my classroom as an example when discussing core elements of identity, culture, diversity, and inclusion. Generally, the conversation starts with a discussion of the physical differences of people and then moves into the invisible differences of culture: rules of engagement, a culture's relationship to nature, socially acceptable ways of interacting, notions of justice, decision making, working styles, and more. More often than I would like to admit, a large majority of time, conversations about cultural differences (whether in a classroom or organizational setting) focus on physical differences and race and ethnicity as the core of culture. I have to remind managers and leaders that subcultures exist, as well as invisible things they do not see, including individual beliefs and assumptions that contribute to the creation of culture.

It is hard for human beings not to categorize because labels help us relate to the world. Ruth Hubbard,[1] an American scientist, said that language helps us to categorize our feelings and thoughts. In this way, we come to understand what is real in our world. These thoughts and feelings set the context for the ways in which we see the world. They frame our thinking and structure our behaviors. George Lakoff[2] wrote that every word in our thinking "evokes a frame" that has been embedded in the brain over long periods of time. Speaking or thinking about the words and images strengthens the neural circuit and reinforces the frame. Although much of what we know and what we have learned came from our early childhood, our thinking continues to be shaped through daily verbal and nonverbal communication and interactions. When we see something that disrupts our frame, our reaction is to protect ourselves and our ways of knowing—anything we can do to reinforce our frame.

There have been numerous times when I have stood in line—in a grocery store, a movie theater, a bank, or a retail store—and the person before or after me becomes visibly upset when a person (usually from a different ethnic group) cuts into the line. "Those people! Don't they know what a line is?" Yet, in other situations, I hear, "That person just cut in line. Oh well." Depending on one's frame—in this case, a cultural frame—standing in a line may or may not be a cultural norm. Your response to the disruption (the image of someone cutting in line) reinforces your frame. You can react with any of the following emotions: anger, surprise, disappointment, rage, or impatience. Alternatively, you may simply ignore it.

Cultural frameworks have a significant impact on how we express ourselves. I frequently tell managers and leaders that we need to learn how to shift our paradigms when working with cultural differences. When we shift, we not only see a different perspective, we are transformed in the process. Margaret Wheatley calls this system shift "emergence," which she describes as "a sudden appearance of a new insight, a new system, and a new capacity."[3] The process is about "stepping outside" and "standing apart" from our world views. When we emerge, we see our thought patterns and habits that form. In this process, we choose to let go of old, inactive learning. Consciously, we choose to participate in continuously learning by adapting to the changing nature of our environments.

Cultural intelligence (CI) principles help to facilitate awareness for, and understanding of, cultural frames. When applied, they bring our frameworks to a conscious level. At a level where we can see the frames, we can then identify what it will take to learn new patterns of thought—new ways to reframe. Reframing, according to Lakoff, "requires a rewiring of the brain. That may take an investment of time, effort, and money."[4] To be culturally intelligent is to reframe or rewire your brain. You create new patterns and new frames by suspending your judgments and assumptions, by considering the old patterns in the face of the new or unfamiliar, and by choosing to change your behavior and attitudes based on reflection and new interpretation. Cultural intelligence is the openness to emergence, not just about the unfamiliar and new culture but about you—who you are and who you could become.

Why This Book?

Peter Drucker,[5] the famous scholar of management, said that we are in an "age of social transformation," a period of our lives where social order is drastically transforming the human condition and what it means from what we have previously known it to be. This age requires us to reflect differently than before on our relationships, on how we resolve intercultural and social conflicts, and on the consequences our actions produce when we are not mindful of our intentions. Similarly, Daniel Pink,[6] in *A Whole New Mind*, speaks about a conceptual age where empathy and emotional intelligence are essential in business; where stories and storytelling are powerful tools to create unity, develop trust, and resolve unsettled business; and where using play can help us find life's meaning and a deeper alignment to our core values.

The changes we see in societies around the globe necessitate a new and different paradigm for how we come to think about culture. All this makes it harder and more challenging to think and practice cultural competence in the same way. Gardner[7] says we need to approach the challenges that differences bring through acceptance, respect, and learning—a frame that he calls the "respectful mind." We must engage in intercultural situations and activities fully; we need to immerse ourselves and experience the "flow"[8] in order to harness the emotions needed to perform and learn from our cultural interactions. Leaders must be willing to explore and create new ways of thinking and interacting with the flow of culture.

In this age of social transformation, cultural intelligence is a topic of urgency for organizational leaders. I hear it from leaders and managers, and I see it in everyday organizational life. Environmental, political, and technological factors are quickly shifting the ways we work and inter-relate with one another. Culture shifts are happening at a faster rate than organizations are ready for and capable of managing, thus creating mental and emotional havoc in managing and leading through cultural transitions. In many cases, the result is a tighter hold on the invisible aspects of culture and stronger emphasis for "the 'right' way to do the work."

More and more, people ask for the tools and information that help carry them through intercultural and cross-cultural interactions. There are a multitude of tools and methodologies that are useful for managing and leading on a global level—the cultural intelligence framework is one of them. It is only one component in the equation for improving the management and leadership of cultural interactions. I tell leaders, "You need to recognize that no matter what tool or method you use, who you are and how you use the tool or method is the biggest part of the equation."

The information in this book is designed to help you understand a piece of that equation. The ideas behind cultural intelligence help you to grasp the important impact of cultural interactions while assisting in your practice as a culturally intelligent leader. Even if you have worked with cultural intelligence or other intercultural communication tools and principles, this book serves as a tool to further develop your proficiency.

Who Is This Book For?

This book is written for leaders who want to learn about cultural intelligence and its application to leadership. Leaders emerge from all walks of life, in formal and informal ways, and notions of leadership differ among cultures. This book uses the definition of leadership from the GLOBE study of leadership across cultures: *the ability of an individual to influence, motivate, and enable others to contribute toward the effectiveness and success of the organizations of which they are members.*[9] People who engage in this process are called leaders.

The model of cultural intelligence is a research-based model that I have used in my consulting and education work with executives, leaders, administrators, boards of directors, students, volunteers, parents, and more. Whether you are in government or in a nonprofit or private sector business, the cultural intelligence framework is practical enough to help you create organizational growth and change. The model speaks to a diverse audience base, and its theoretical foundations are useful to those who want to learn more about the scientific elements of culture.

Reading the Book

This book outlines the importance of understanding culture and its impact on our lives, the strategic value of cultural intelligence, and the significance of integrating and practicing cultural intelligence in everyday life. The book is designed to help you overcome the challenges in intercultural interactions by focusing on cultural intelligence in leadership and management.

This book does not focus on specific cultural etiquettes or how to do business in other countries. It is a book designed to help you apply cultural intelligence to any cultural situation. This is not an academic textbook, although the concepts presented here are essential to your knowledge about culture and intercultural interactions.

The eight chapters in this book consist of reflection exercises and case studies that can be used as a guide to your continued learning and development in cultural intelligence. Each chapter begins with a personal story, quote, or idea about culture and intercultural work and ends with a summary of the key concepts. To continue your work in cultural intelligence, there is a website (www.cileadership.com) that has been set up to provide you with more sample case studies and inventories.

- The *Introduction* provides an overview to the topic of cultural intelligence. It examines globalization and its significance for culturally intelligent leadership.

- *Chapter 1* explores the literature on culture and leadership. It examines several studies that illustrate the importance of understanding culture in leadership and management.
- *Chapter 2* examines the concept of culture. The chapter focuses on recognizing the different levels of culture and how culture is shared and learned. It also highlights the significance of cultural value dimensions in intercultural work.
- *Chapter 3* focuses on what cultural intelligence is and what it consists of. It describes how cultural intelligence is different from other forms of intelligences.
- *Chapter 4* delves into the first component of cultural intelligence: cultural strategic thinking. It focuses on the topics of cognition and metacognition. Techniques and tools to practice and improve metacognition are offered.
- *Chapter 5* moves into a discussion of motivation and mindfulness, the second part to cultural intelligence. The chapter centers on the role of self-efficacy in culture and the value mindfulness has in intercultural interactions.
- *Chapter 6* focuses on the third component of cultural intelligence: behavior. It focuses on the notion of self-concept and how this impacts behavior and attitudes. Additionally, this section examines the impact of behavioral communication.
- *Chapter 7* consists of 10 case studies that illustrate different cultural situations. It provides you with the opportunity to practice the cultural intelligence principles.
- *Chapter 8* looks into the future and examines what is needed for cultural intelligence principles to thrive. It also discusses the types of leadership needed to bring more attention to cultural intelligence.

You can read this book in the following ways:

- *Begin at the beginning.* If you would like to understand cultural intelligence and its relationship to culture in depth, I recommend starting at the beginning and reading the book sequentially. The book is written as if you were taking a workshop in cultural intelligence; it begins with a basic foundation to culture before delving into principles of cultural intelligence.

- *Read individual chapters.* Cultural intelligence principles overlap with each other. In this book, each cultural intelligence principle is discussed separately in its own chapter so you can choose which chapter to focus on. But each chapter is written in a way that helps you connect that principle to other principles of cultural intelligence.

- *Read case studies and work on inventories.* If you would like to use cultural intelligence as a training tool, you can visit the website www.cileadership.com for a list of inventories and updated case studies.

Definitions and Terminology

Throughout the book, the following terms will be used. Sometimes they are used interchangeably, sometimes alone, and sometimes together. Additionally, this book makes a clear distinction between management and leadership and managers and leaders, a difference that is outlined in chapter 1.

Culture: shared beliefs, values, and assumptions of a group of people who learn from one another and teach others that their behaviors, attitudes, and perspectives are the correct ways to think, act, and feel.[10]

Cross-Cultural: involving two or more cultures

Diversity: *distinct and unlike elements or qualities* (interests, people, ideas, perspectives, ability, region, etc.); can be visible and invisible

Intercultural: *between or among people of different cultures*

Intracultural: *within the same culture*

Multicultural: *many or several cultures*

Intercultural competence: ability to successfully interact with people of different cultural backgrounds

We are living in exciting times that call for courageous and authentic leadership in navigating through blurred boundaries. The changes we see are opportunities for growth and development as individuals, organizations, and communities. We have an opportunity to identify and clarify our interpretation of the world through our relationships with one another. We can seize the chance to identify our blind spots and to uncover the stories we tell about ourselves and why we can or cannot interact with others. We have the potential to explore our work around cultures in a way that uncovers the hidden routines and habitual behaviors that contribute negatively to human relationships.

INTRODUCTION

A Global Community

When I left Minnesota in the 1990s to attend college on the east coast, I was excited because I knew that I would experience a multitude of cultures that did not exist or were barely visible in Minnesota. In an urban setting like Minneapolis and St. Paul, it was not uncommon to enter a Target store or visit a museum or a local library and see that Minnesota was primarily inhabited by people of northern European origin. In the past 20 years, Minnesota, much like the rest of the United States, has reflected a global community. Refugees and immigrants are coming from all over the world—West and East Africa, Southeast Asia, Russia and Bosnia, Central and South America, and the Middle East—and contributing to the economic system.

I noticed this change when I returned to Minnesota after my studies. I remember dropping my siblings off at their high school and seeing for the first time a group of high school girls wearing the *hijab*, a head covering, and the *jilbab*, the dress coat. I could not take my eyes off them. I had read books and magazine articles and seen pictures of women with the hijab on the evening news. I was used to seeing these images, yet I was completely transfixed with the actual experience of seeing the pictures come to life only 100 feet away from me. I wondered, what was their story? How did they come to the United States? Did they like wearing the hijab? Was it a choice?

Soon after this experience I became more aware of the East African population in the Twin Cities. I noticed them when I was standing in line at the grocery store, the library, and the bank. I began to hear stories on the evening news about the resettlement challenges they faced as new immigrants, which reminded me of my own. Eventually, I worked alongside them and learned about their cultural history and life in the U.S. Through these intercultural experiences, I learned in my early 20s that although culture can shape people to have different beliefs and values, different language and customs, the globalization of societies was quickly forcing us to work and live together in ways we had not done before. It is making us more aware of who we are, our differences, and how we relate to others.

In *The World Is Flat*, Thomas Friedman[1] describes forces that are flattening the world and creating a convergence of many systems into one. These forces include the spread of information technology, online collaborative communities, and offshoring and outsourcing, among others. These factors are changing our social environment and redefining the ways in which we interact with one another. We do not need to fly across the globe to experience national cultural shifts—they come to us, no matter where we live. This is a familiar picture across the United States, but it is not unique to U.S. citizens. Even in countries like India and China, which are experiencing phenomenal economic growth, globalization has altered their lifestyles. As an example, my colleague in China gets up either very early or stays up very late into the night for her business meetings with clients in the United States. Owning a business and working globally has limited her social life to business events and networking. She hardly has time for her family and she feels guilty that she is not the traditional Chinese daughter and mother.

My colleague, like many others around the world doing business globally, is learning to cope with cultural shifts. A few years ago I attended a leadership conference where I met Betsy, who had lived and worked in the Midwest for all her life. At that time she worked for a U.S. company and was part of a management team supervising a customer service division in Bangalore. As we talked about the challenges of working in a multicultural, global team, Betsy shared with me that her employees in India were fascinated with Americans and especially wanted to learn how to speak more "American." I asked her what she meant about "speaking more American" and she replied,

"They want to know American slang and how we pronounce words. They are motivated to want to learn to speak better English without an accent."

"Why is it important for them to speak without an accent?" I asked.

"It helps the customers." She said. Betsy explained further, "Customers in the U.S. feel better if they speak to someone who doesn't have an accent. They feel like they're speaking to someone right here in the U.S. instead of thousands of miles away in a different part of the world."

Her comment made me ask, "Do you think that they could do their job well even with an accent?" Betsy's response was, "Of course! It's just that it's easier if the customer can understand. It's also true for our team members here in the U.S. They get frustrated when they don't understand their Indian coworkers. For some people the accent really is a distraction. They just give up."

Then I said to her, "If you have a problem understanding them, don't you think that your Indian workforce in India also has problems understanding the way you talk? It seems to me that your staff in India is really motivated to adapt, and I wonder if you think your team here in the U.S. can be just as adaptable?"

Betsy pondered that for a moment, and then said, "Sure. It's easy to say that we can be adaptable but actually doing it is very hard."

I replied, "I think it's hard for everyone."

I walked away from that conversation thinking that global changes will only increase, especially in countries like China and India, and that Betsy and her team would be better equipped for the future if they could learn to be more adaptable. James Canton, a social scientist and global futurist, predicts that global changes will create an "innovation economy." He wrote, "Already, every economy—local, regional, national, or global—is deeply affected by innovation. Those effects will multiply a thousand fold over the next fifty years."[2] This innovation economy includes the following characteristics and trends:

- Development of new manufacturing processes to enable faster, on-demand production
- New communication systems that connect people to information in real time
- Creation of information services that are translatable into software, games, and programs that provide greater customer value to consumers and businesses
- Development of materials that are smarter, safer, and cleaner to make into products

- A focus on developing renewable, clean, and affordable fuels
- Discovery of new methods to increase the ability of individuals and companies to be more mobile and reach more customers[3]

These changes demand that organizations create new skill sets and knowledge; they require leaders and organizations to create work environments that support the new innovation economy. The trends in the innovation economy, like any system, have an effect on global demographic changes. The following are factors that will shape the work force:

- Hispanics and women will dominate the U.S. work force.
- Women will comprise a high percentage of new workers and leaders.
- Increased immigration will be necessary to enable available talent to keep up with the demands of business and society.
- The future work force will not be defined by geography; rather, it will be defined by talent.
- The aging population in America and Europe will have dramatic effects on society and the economy.
- Innovation will be a key driver of work force skills, requiring an overhaul of the education system.[4]

The next list consists of statistics that point to additional changes in the global economy; these are expediting the need for intercultural understanding and awareness:

- The United States exported US$1.57 trillion in goods and services in 2009.[5]
- Hispanics or Latinos, Blacks or African Americans, and Asians continue to increase their share of the labor force[6] and are projected to be doing so faster than their White counterparts.
- Between 1992 and 2012, the increase in the labor force for African American women will be 39.6%, for Asian Americans, 75.7%, and for Latina Americans, 109.8%.[7]
- Factors impacting the composition and growth of the labor force over the next 50 years will include the baby-boomer

generation, the stabilization of the women's labor force, and increasing racial and ethnic diversity in the work force.[8]

- Increased immigration rates will further diversify the U.S. population and labor force.[9]
- The 2010 U.S. Census estimates that the "nation's minority population is steadily rising and now makes up 35 percent of the United States, advancing an unmistakable trend that could make minorities the new American majority by midcentury."[10]

All of this information, along with international migration, the restructuring of jobs and organizations, and international market expansion, means that "as economic borders come down, cultural barriers go up presenting new challenges and opportunities in business; when cultures come into contact, they may converge on some aspects, but their idiosyncrasies will likely amplify."[11] Take for example the following:

Joan is the president of a Chamber of Commerce located in the Midwest. As part of their ongoing work, they need to partner with local businesses to discuss a multi-million-dollar commercial revitalization project proposed by the city. Many of the local business owners in the district are Hispanic, and their business would be severely affected by the changes. Joan's association has partnered in the past with some of the businesses for association events, but not a lot of collaboration has occurred between the Chamber and the Hispanic business owners. It's essential that the Chamber meet and discuss potential barriers to the project with the Hispanic community.

Joan identifies specific Hispanic business owners to partner with in hopes that they would help bring in other members of their community. Early in the partnership Joan encounters problems. It takes her several times to secure a meeting with four business owners in the district. When the first meeting is scheduled, two of the owners were late and one never showed up.

Because the meeting started late, Joan quickly facilitates introductions, and then moves on to discussing the proposed changes from the city and the impact it could have on business owners. She moves quickly through the agenda items, helping the group to stay on task and focused on the purpose of the meeting. In the end, the group decides to meet again to discuss the proposal. When it comes time again for their second meeting, no one shows up.

For Joan, time is running out. The city wants to hear how the Chamber will help the Hispanic business owners with the new proposal. After several attempts to connect with the business owners, Joan finds out from other sources that the business owners do not trust the Chamber. The owners do not feel the Chamber knows what is important to the Hispanic community. Joan is surprised. The purpose for the first meeting was to establish trust and to build a relationship with the community, which she thought they did. Joan doesn't understand how a meeting could set off a chain of reactions like this.

Both Joan and the Hispanic business owners come to a meeting to discuss a commercial revitalization project. Although having a meeting to discuss business is standard in both cultures, how a meeting is conducted, what is discussed, and who talks first at a meeting are all idiosyncrasies of culture. Because Joan is not aware of the cultural idiosyncrasies, it is hard for her to understand and correct the situation. Even if she did not know the specific cultural facts of how to conduct and interact in meetings with Hispanic business owners, she could still adapt to the situation by being present in the moment and noticing the verbal and nonverbal cues of her colleagues. All this points to the need for leaders to be culturally intelligent when working with one another, whether it is on a local, regional, national, or international level.

Leaders cannot afford to make mistakes in business due to cultural differences. Joan's mistake was being unaware of the cultural differences between herself and her Hispanic colleagues. This lack of awareness and understanding led her to behave in a way that was culturally inappropriate, leading to consequences that would impact her organization. Even with Betsy and her multicultural team, cultural barriers such as language can play a large role in the success or failure of her global team. The recognition of cultural challenges is essential even when a group appears to be homogenous. Paying attention to the idiosyncrasies will likely enable a leader to make different choices that contribute to the effectiveness of a team and organization. Not considering cultural differences can lead to the loss of sales and contracts, damaged reputations, and broken partnerships, as in the example of Joan and the Chamber of Commerce. These are just some of the consequences of intercultural misunderstandings.

Working in a global community means that leaders must learn to overcome cultural differences in the following ways:

1. **Understand cultural differences and their manifestations**. Throughout the course of my work in diversity and leadership, I meet leaders who encounter challenges, big and small, related to cultural differences. The ones I found to effectively lead through the differences were those who took the initiative to understand differences and how they played out among individuals, team members, and organizations. For example, John, the chief of police for a city in Alabama, told me that one thing he helps his employees to understand is the pervasiveness of culture. He constantly reminds them that a person's individual culture can impact the entire culture of a team and organization. He said, "What happens to a person one day can change that person's perspective and belief. If this person comes into this organization and interacts with their peers and this person is in a leadership position, you better believe that the rest of his peers will begin to believe what he believes. That's my challenge. Every day I tell my directors they need to lead through the challenges."

2. **Be able to transfer cultural knowledge from one culture to another**. I find that culturally intelligent leaders are those that take the time to know about a culture. They look for opportunities to learn about the cultural facts, the music, the history, the language, and the behaviors of people within the culture. They tell others about what they have learned, thus helping them to remember the information and verbalize their experiences. Most importantly, they use the information gained to help them understand themselves and their own cultural upbringing. By doing this, they are able to adapt from one culture to another.

3. **Recognize their biases, assumptions, and cultural frameworks**. When leaders are able to identify and recognize their cultural biases and assumptions, it helps them to let go of preconceived ideas. The

ability to do this helps leaders to identify the elements of their thinking that get in the way of culturally intelligent behaviors. I learned that culturally intelligent leaders take the time to reflect on their biases and assumptions; they use mistakes and failures as opportunities to improve. I once consulted with a senior director who told me that the more she practiced thinking about her thinking, the more it enabled her to learn about herself and her reactions to situations.

4. **Be motivated and committed to working through cultural conflicts**. Intercultural conflicts are extremely challenging but not impossible to work through. The times I found success in conflict resolution among team members or a manager and employee were when both parties were willing and motivated to discuss the conflict, even when it seemed that the process was at a standstill. As an example, I worked with a director and her employee to help them understand each other's working style to enable them to work better together. At the end of an emotionally charged session the director committed herself to continuing the dialogue. Additionally, she committed resources to help both of them learn more about each other. The director's expression of her commitment modeled the way for the employee to do the same.

5. **Be willing to adapt and learn to live and work with different cultures**. I am always amazed at the ability of human and organizational systems to be adaptive and resilient. A leader's positive attitude toward change and flexibility propels him or her further along the cultural intelligence continuum than a negative one. For example, when I worked with Susan and Megan, both directors looking for my help to implement diversity workshops, I noticed that Susan always had a positive approach to thinking about culture, and it showed up in the words she used. She would say, "I'm optimistic" or "It will be a challenge but I know that we can make this work." Whereas Megan *seemed* optimistic about the work, but you could hear seeds of doubt in her words. She would say, "It's a challenge and I am not sure how we can make it work." At one point Susan was quite frustrated and told Megan that if they did not try to make a change, they would remain in the situation with the same problems. What turned Megan around was her willingness to move

toward adaptation; her attitude changed and as a result, both directors became models of working with change.

In an innovation economy, leaders will need to be culturally intelligent. The demographic changes of societies, including the make-up of the work force, require leaders to gain new skills and knowledge that help them to maintain an ideology of change and adaptation. To be competent in global cultures is no longer the norm; it is a requirement for leaders to cultivate their competence into cultural intelligence. It is more than competence, which is having the abilities to function or develop in specific ways. It is about knowing how to use the abilities and making sense of them in cultural situations. Cultural intelligence (CI) can be used to help leaders work through intercultural dilemmas and create understanding and awareness across and between cultures. In the new innovation economy, leaders must be familiar with the basic principles of intercultural interaction and communication, and they must be able to teach and pass on this knowledge to those they lead. In this way, leaders embrace and perform cultural intelligence in their daily lives.

Chapter Summary

- Globalization is flattening the world and has created changes to our social and political environments.
- Lifestyle changes are happening all around the world.
- Technological changes are creating an "innovation economy" that will require new skill sets and knowledge, and new organizational structures.
- Demographic changes in the work force are affecting intercultural work. The most important changes include an aging baby boomer generation, increasing immigration, a growing Hispanic population in the United States, and more women participating in the work force.
- Cultural challenges and value conflicts will naturally occur as economic boundaries disappear.
- Culturally intelligent leaders are needed to resolve intercultural issues and find solutions for working with one another.

CHAPTER 1

Culturally Intelligent Leadership Matters

The first time I taught cultural intelligence principles to a group of executives in Minnesota, I miscalculated the time. I did not have the conference coordinator's e-mail or phone number, which was useless to me anyway since my cell phone froze.

When I arrived at the site, the entire parking lot was packed with cars, and so were the side streets and adjacent parking areas for at least a four-block radius. When I finally found a parking space, I hurriedly picked up the large box in the back of my car that held my training materials. By the time I reached the conference room, I was tired and sweaty from walking in my 3-inch-high-heeled pumps. The coordinator was anxiously awaiting my arrival. Even though I profusely apologized for being late, she gave me "a look" that said, "how unprofessional."

As I entered the room, all eyes were on me, of course. Everyone was on time, and I, as the trainer, should have been there before the first person entered the room. Any reason I provided would have been a terrible excuse for this particular crowd, made up of professionals dressed in their business suits, with pens and paper in hand, ready to learn. They paid a lot of money for the conference, of which I was teaching only one half-day session.

What went through my mind as I set up my materials, quickly handing them out to the participants? *I messed up. Wow, this is really bad and unprofessional. They are not bringing me back, for sure. Those people in the corner look mad. At least that woman over there seems sympathetic—or was that a facial twitch?*

"Good morning," I said. "Thank you for coming. I see you're all early. And now that we've had the chance to get to know each other, let's begin the training." You can imagine the facial expressions I received from the audience: confusion, disbelief, bewilderment.

"Oh, I'm sorry. Is there something wrong with what I said? Let me explain. You all arrived here on time, as Americans generally would. I also arrived here on time, as a Hmong person would. You just happened to be on American time, and I'm following Hmong time. You might think I'm late, but in Hmong time, I'm actually quite early." That broke the ice for the group, and I decided to use the experience to lead into the session about cultural intelligence.

"Since all of you were here really early, I'm sure you had the chance to introduce yourselves; find out about each other's families, where you're from, who you're related to, right? No? Well, that's not right. We can't start the training if you haven't had the chance to relax and just learn about each other. We better do that or else we're going to face some problems later."

The experience was the perfect opportunity to share and discuss the challenges involved in navigating cultural terrains. Turning my personal experience into a "teaching moment" gave the audience the chance to pause and reflect about the differences in cultural expression and behavior. The example was used to help the participants dig deeper and to draw out their Western, cultural assumptions. They learned to ask questions like the following:

- What are the differences in time between her culture and mine?
- How do Hmong people approach meetings and trainings?
- Is this behavior specific to the trainer, as an individual, regardless of her national culture?
- Is this behavior specific to her family and how she was raised?
- Why do I care if she was "late"?
- Can I let go of my emotional attachment for her be here "on time"?
- What am I not seeing in this situation?
- What is my motivation for resolving this situation?
- How am I behaving? Do I need to change my behavior? If so, what can I do?

Why are these questions important to ask? Asking the questions that move you away from immediate reaction to positive action and reflection is necessary in cultural intelligence work. It enables you to have an awareness of the idiosyncrasies of culture, the peculiarities of its effects, and the role it plays in our lives. When you are able to accomplish this, you create a new awareness of your surroundings—you create a new picture of the situation. The practice of creating new awareness and understanding is your ability to be adaptable and flexible.

In the *Tao te Ching*, an ancient Chinese manuscript written by Lao-tzu and translated by Stephen Mitchell,[1] Lao Tzu explains how one can live his or her life in perfect harmony with conflicting forces. He writes throughout the book about the importance of a person's ability to be flexible and adaptable. At birth, he says, we are all malleable. As we grow older, knowledge that we gain from our social and cultural environments often leads us to become rigid and blocked. Lao-tzu says that flexibility is essential to growth and evolution, and that we need to choose adaptability over rigidity for survival.

In a world where organizations must be change-focused, adaptable, and flexible in their intercultural work, leaders are being asked to help people work through, and come to terms with, the changes that differences often bring. Organizations and leaders that expect change tend to thrive—they anticipate and envision different scenarios of environmental change, both internally and externally.[2] Leaders who are bound to a single viewpoint or perspective are no longer effective when leading because the perspectives narrow the opportunities for sustainable organizational growth. When leaders are focused on change and embrace an adaptability mindset, they can be better informed, make the right decisions, and provide the right resources to motivate their employees to succeed and perform at their best levels.

The Difference Between Managers and Leaders

Warren Bennis famously wrote in his book *On Becoming a Leader* that a manager does things right and leaders do the right thing.[3] Like other leadership scholars, Bennis makes a clear distinction between leadership and management and between managers and leaders. A manager's behavior and activities focus on controlling, planning, coordinating, and organizing. This differs from a leader, whose behaviors and tasks focus on innovation, vision, motivation, trust, and change.[4]

Table 1.1. Difference Between Management and Leadership

Managers	Leaders
Cope with *complexity* by . . . • planning for goals • budgeting for goals • establishing agendas and tasks • organizing roles and responsibilities • structuring staff and jobs • delegating people • monitoring and implementing results • identifying deviations • planning and organizing to solve problems	Cope with *change* by . . . • setting direction • developing a future • having a strategic vision for change • aligning of people • communicating direction • creating coalitions • being commitment focused • motivating and inspiring • leveraging human value and potential

Note. Adapted from Kotter, *What Leaders Really Do* (1999). Cambridge, MA: Harvard Business Review.

Cultural intelligence requires leadership, not management. It calls for what Ronald Heifetz[5] defines as courageous leadership, that is, the courage to see reality and help others see their realities: the realities of who they are, how they behave, what talents and skill sets they have or are missing in this global world, and what opportunities should be capitalized upon and seized. Leaders must be able to see and anticipate what skill sets are needed in the future, not just develop their employees' skills for the moment.[6]

Culturally intelligent leaders must create an environment where diversity and culture flourish, and where conflicting values can be safely expressed and explored through dialogue. Barry Salzberg, CEO of Deloitte, says that organizations and leaders must ask themselves the hard questions: Does our corporate culture really accept the differences it invites, and do we really embrace the different perspectives that come from increasing our commitment to recruiting?[7] This type of perspective demands leaders who work toward transformation, or what Couto calls *citizen leaders*, "transforming leaders who engage others in efforts to reach higher levels of human awareness and relationships."[8]

Importance of Leadership in a Global Economy

Over the years, leadership scholars have found in their studies that, when talking about the leadership process, culture matters.[9] In general, the leadership literature points to the critical need for cross-cultural and global leadership, especially given the pressing need to build networks and relationships[10] and to create an appreciation for differences and similarities. Bennis noted that, although leadership competencies have remained the same, "our understanding of what it is and how it works and the ways in which people learn to apply it has shifted."[11]

Leadership theories and models available thus far, while helpful in understanding leadership development, are inadequate paradigms for a full understanding of the changing nature of leadership in the 21st century. Goldsmith et al.[12] argued for new forms of leadership that include thinking globally, appreciating cultural diversity, developing technological savvy, building partnerships and alliances, and sharing leadership. Research into cross-cultural leadership revealed that understanding national cultures is critical to leadership development and that organizations must accept differing perceptions of leadership.[13]

Leadership theories and programs that operate from a Western-based, androcentric framework hinder the shift that is required for understanding leadership on a broader level. Situational leadership theories,[14] which focus on leadership traits, skills, and styles, are inadequate models in this regard because their basic foundation (understanding the individual as leader) implies a Western-based ideology of leadership that does not exist in many national cultures; therefore, the underlying concepts of this style of leadership do not always translate universally. Other theories, such as transformational and team leadership, emphasize the collective voice as essential yet neglect the cultural implications for leadership. Even cultures that share similar Western beliefs about organizational structure still operate differently based on their unique cultural contexts.[15]

In a global economy, it is becoming increasingly more important to understand the wants and needs of those we serve, that is, the internal and external stakeholders. Having awareness of this need means that leaders must be able to shape the culture of their organizations to address changing stakeholder needs. Edgar Schein noted that leaders can do this by having a "personal sense that they are the creation of the cultures of the countries, families, occupations, and reference groups, and that culture plays a huge role in the capacities of their organization to form."[16] Culturally intelligent leaders need be strategic in aligning the culture of their organizations with the people who work in them. This organizational culture becomes an advantage for leaders, making it easier for them to respond to external environmental factors, which include culture shifts.

Debbe Kennedy[17] proposed the following five qualities that leaders need in order to address and use cultural differences to the advantage of their organization:

- *Leaders must make diversity a priority.*
- *Leaders must get to know people and their differences.*
- *Leaders must enable rich communication.*
- *Leaders must make accountability a core value.*
- *Leaders must be able to establish mutualism as the final arbiter.*

These five characteristics I have seen as important differences between the ways that managers and leaders handle cultural conflicts and situations. Culturally intelligent leaders are those that elevate diversity to the top of organizational planning and view it as a critical factor to innovation and creativity. Innovation in diversity begins with a definition of diversity, which many organizations lack or have poorly articulated. If they do, diversity definitions are focused on race and ethnicity and do not explore the dynamic dimensions implicit in culture. In a 2007 study on diversity in the workplace, the Society of Human Resource Management[18] reported that only 30% of organizations have a shared definition of diversity within their organization. However, 75% feel that diversity can be used to improve work and relationships. A focus for, and an articulation of, defining diversity and its importance in the work force can open dialogue for organizations.

Having culturally intelligent leaders in organizations matters because they help to develop a curiosity for differences in the workplace in employees. They help to provide access to information and intentionally gather cultural knowledge on a daily basis that will help them and others learn more about differences and the influence of differences in the workplace. Additionally, leaders can foster creativity and curiosity when they set aside some time, on a day-to-day basis, to practice and master their cultural intelligence skills.

When I have seen culturally intelligent leaders in action, they cultivate an environment of trust, which is critical when working with differences in the workplace. Patrick Lencioni[19] wrote that trust is a critical foundational element in interpersonal relationships. Leaders must be willing to be vulnerable in intercultural interactions, openly admitting what they know and don't know about culture and cultural differences. They must be able to admit that they might not be able to resolve intercultural differences. By demonstrating vulnerability, a leader enables richer communication and creates an inviting space and environment for intercultural dialogue. In this situation, people are more willing to ask for help and to provide one another with constructive feedback; they take risks and learn to appreciate the differences in skills and style that each person brings to the work environment.

For diversity and culture to flourish in organizations, everyone in the workplace must hold each other accountable toward differences. My experiences working with leaders of different sectors, both formal and informal, have shown me that the creation of a mission and vision for diversity can only take an organization so far. Culturally Intelligent leaders create standards of accountability, explaining what is expected of each employee and of themselves in intercultural interactions.

As an example, I was brought in to facilitate a workshop about cultural differences for public sector employees. In this workshop, the city manager and a city council member were present; they wanted to demonstrate to their employees the importance of culture and their commitment to diversity in the city. At the end of the session, they stood up and addressed the participants, reminding them that the workshop they participated in was only one of many to come. Moreover, the city manager and city council member told the employees that they would do whatever it took to ensure that everyone was held accountable for delivering culturally relevant services to the department's clients. In this way, "Putting differences to work is greatly enhanced when personal responsibility is a common thread woven tightly into everyone's fabric."[20]

When everyone is held accountable for their choices and behaviors in an intercultural workplace, there is a higher level of respect and trust among workers. Everyone is encouraged to perform his or her best and to hold themselves to the highest standards in working with each other. Intercultural conflicts still occur, but the responses to these conflicts from individuals are different.

Lee Bolman and Terrence Deal[21] wrote that organizations are a coalition of individuals and groups with different interests, preferences, and beliefs. The differences among individuals and groups can change, but this usually occurs very slowly. Leaders must be able to identify mutual interests, values, and beliefs in order to create a culture of mutual interdependence. Because conflict is unavoidable, and often necessary, it is best for leaders to create a picture of mutual dependence that is both beneficial and progressive for employees.

Leadership matters even more when cultures are intertwined in the workplace. Leadership and culture are like two pieces of rope. On their own, they can be used to bundle objects, connect one thing to another, and even support weight. When threaded and intertwined, they do all of these things but are much stronger and have a lower chance of being snapped. A rope is firm and strong yet flexible and pliable. Because change is constant, leaders can use their cultural intelligence to steer organizations, and those they lead, toward finding innovative strategies and solutions to intercultural issues.

Like an anthropologist, culturally intelligent leaders explore, discover, and find cultural artifacts in their business environment that are both barriers to, and promoters of, growth. A culturally intelligent leader will accomplish this from an "outsider" perspective while keeping his or her "insider" perspective in line. Ronald Heifetz[22] says that one should take a leap to get a balcony perspective when one has been on the dance floor too long; this enables one to see a bigger picture of what is really going on in the intercultural business workplace. Reminding yourself that what you see is only one perspective of a bigger picture can help you to pay attention to what you did not notice or what you cannot see. Cultural intelligence requires leaders to take a critical role in guiding different values in order to bring them into alignment with the business. However, leaders need not do this alone; in fact, they should invite and encourage members to assist in addressing diversity and then challenge them to be culturally intelligent as well.

Chapter Summary

- Culturally intelligent leaders are change-focused and change-ready. They anticipate different scenarios for change and enable their organizations and people to embrace change.
- Many leadership scholars differentiate between management and leadership and managers and leaders.
- Managers are responsible for controlling, coordinating, planning, and organizing. Leaders are people who inspire, motivate, unite people, and create visions for the future.
- Cultural intelligence requires leadership and leaders, not management and managers.
- Historically, leadership theories and frameworks are based on Western ideologies and perspectives.
- Leadership theories and frameworks must incorporate a global perspective that considers differences in perceptions of leadership and leaders.
- Leaders must be able to create cultures where differences thrive. They may accomplish this by: making diversity a priority, getting to know people and their differences, enabling trust, holding each person accountable for differences, and establishing mutual interdependence.
- Leadership and culture are intertwined like two halves of a rope threaded together. At times, leaders must be able to step away from what they are experiencing to understand the full impact of culture on leadership.

CHAPTER 2

Understanding Culture

When my parents came to the United States in 1979, their world became vastly different than what they had known. Before their arrival, they lived in a small hilltop, tribal village in the mountains of Laos, like many of their ancestors before them. They had the simplest tools for doing their work and for living their lives. The natural world provided everything they needed. If they wanted to use the bathroom, they went outside—not to an outhouse but to the woods. When they were hungry, they cooked the meal in a pot over a large fire pit. When relatives asked them to attend celebrations and notified them that the celebration meal would begin sometime when the sun was to set, my parents knew that the path of the sun would let them know when they should leave their house.

There were a lot of assumptions my parents made about their world. When they had to relocate to the United States, they found out how different their assumptions were when they were tested in an environment that contradicted their ways of being. They were not aware of a different way of living their lives, because the norms that shaped their lives influenced their actions and behaviors. The norms helped them to learn that what they did was the correct way to live.

One of their most difficult challenges was to unlearn what they knew in a different context and with different materials and tools that they did not have before. What naturally occurred was a process of culture shock and then a period of acculturation. When my parents' sponsors showed them how to use the toilet by gesturing what to do and how to flush, my parents were embarrassed. Coming from a culture where modesty is important, they did not know how to respond to the American sponsor's gestures, yet their embarrassment quickly turned into fascination when they saw how a toilet could dispose of materials.

Interpreting body language became a critical piece of adaptation and learning. My parents found the exaggerated gestures of their sponsors turning on and off the stove "different." But it was paying attention to the facial gestures and body language that helped them to understand how to operate a stove. They realized certain things were the same across cultures: taking out a pot to boil water, placing it on a heated surface for the water to boil, taking the pot off the surface to let the water cool. The differences, they noticed, were in the equipment used and the timing of the water boiling. What a surprise it was for them to realize that one could adjust and control temperature!

As human beings who are accustomed to behaving (consciously and unconsciously) in specific ways, we often do not recognize another perspective until it is presented to us. Ellen Langer,[1] a social psychologist, says that it is in the perspective of another that we learn to see ourselves—to see who we really are. As an educator and facilitator, I meet people in positions of leadership every day who believe that their perspective about culture and how they should work with differences is the right way and that there is no other possibility for a different way of working or thinking. For example, a participant in my training session, Jacob, felt very strongly about the "invasion" (his word, not mine) of immigrants in his neighborhood. As a result, the city he worked for was increasingly diverse and would need to set up services and programs to meet the needs of the new immigrants.

As a native of the city, Jacob felt strongly that his neighbors needed to assimilate more quickly. As a city employee and manager, he felt excluded that the city would create new services for the immigrants. His issue of conflict here was that he had developed proposals for expanding current services in his department, but they were never approved, mostly because of budgetary reasons. He did not understand why creating "special services for a small population" mattered more than the services for current residents of the city, and he was angry that the funds set aside for the new programming would be large, much larger than his proposed changes.

Jacob, in this example, is bound to his single perspective or viewpoint. He cannot see beyond the situation. And, in fact, when discussing this situation with Jacob and other managers present, other pieces of the story began to unravel. Yes, Jacob had a perspective about immigrants based on his experiences with one immigrant—his neighbor. He used his knowledge and interactions with this person to generalize to an entire population. Additionally, what really mattered to him in his place of work was that he did not feel his ideas mattered. Because every time he proposed changes they were not approved, he took that as a deliberate attack on him. This was not the case at all, and he was told this by his peers in the training.

When Jacob was presented with another perspective, he let his guard down. Over time, he was able to focus on the real issue, which was that no matter what your status, creed, ethnicity, or reason for moving to the United States, as a public sector employee it was his role to provide the appropriate services that would meet the residents' needs.

As leaders, we must make strong efforts to see a different perspective than what we believe and hold to be true. We must challenge ourselves, as Byron Katie[2] says, by asking whether we know what we see to be true is really, in fact, true. And if it is, how do we know that? What stories have we told ourselves? To understand this, we need to look at the "roots of culture" and how our cultural systems have shaped our realities of the world.

Cultural Systems

Imagine a tree as a metaphor for a *cultural system*—all the things that make up who you are. The roots of a tree are essential for the survival of the tree. They carry the nutrients needed for the growth of the tree and store nutrients for later feeding. Roots of trees are generally located in the top 6 to 24 inches of the ground, not too deep from the surface. The roots are impacted by their surrounding, and environmental factors contribute to their health and vitality.

Just like the roots on a tree, cultural systems have roots that are impacted by their surroundings. A culture's rituals, traditions, ceremonies, myths, and symbols provide it with the nutrients it needs to survive. Environmental factors can change a tree by uprooting it or letting it die off, making space for new life in its place. Similarly, environmental changes impact cultural systems, forcing it to adapt and change to its surroundings or transition into death, creating new cultural stories that carry new life.

But unlike trees and their roots, we get stuck in our cultural systems and do not budge even when our surroundings have changed. Trees, like anything in an ecosystem, have natural cycles of renewal and rebirth. Sometimes this renewal and rebirth is gradual and gentle, while other times it is fast, disruptive, and violent. Trees, because they share their environments with others, will learn to adapt and allow change to occur, no matter what the direction of change may be. Change in their cultural environments is inevitable and a part of the life cycle.

In similar ways, we can think about our cultural systems as part of a larger system. Some cultural anthropologists would describe the cultural systems as "big C" (macroculture) and "little C" (microculture). The macroculture refers to a larger cultural system, for example, Catholicism is a culture that is not bounded by geography. Within the macroculture of Catholicism are smaller units of culture called *subcultures*. Change is constant in each cultural system, and transitions, renewal, and rebirth are endless cycles. As cultural shifts—small and large, gradual and disruptive—occur in the macro- and microcultures, the entire system learns to adapt in different ways.

What Is Culture?

Definitions of culture cover a wide range of perspectives. When I ask participants in my business workshops to describe culture, the following are words and phrases they use: *food, religion, language, music, region or geography, ethnicity, clothes,* and so on. Generally, there is always one person who raises his or her hand timidly and says, "I think culture is more than that. It's the things we don't see, like our beliefs or views about gender." Both are correct—culture represents the things we see, the tangible, as well as the intangible things.

Figure 2.1. Iceberg metaphor.

The iceberg, a commonly used metaphor to describe culture, is a great example for illustrating the tangible and the intangible. When talking about culture, most people focus on the "tip of the iceberg," which is considered as making up 10% of the object. The rest of the iceberg, 90% of it, is below the waterline. Most leaders in businesses, when addressing intercultural situations, pick up on the things they see—things on the "tip of the iceberg." This means that they never address the cultural issues and problems that are underneath the surface level. Solutions become temporary band-aids covering deeply rooted cultural systems.

I once had a manager describe and define culture as "a monster." After some laughter from the group, he clarified his statement: "It's so messy and sometimes it's too big to handle. And, it's scary because you don't know what you're dealing with." What he said rings true for many people and businesses that work in multicultural settings. It is certainly not fun to clean up cultural messes, bloopers, or misunderstandings, and when not addressed right away, they can result in large cultural conflicts. The ability to acknowledge one's cultural mistakes, and having a commitment to learning what culture brings, is a skill that one must have in cultural intelligence work.

This definition of culture as a "monster" is one that looks at culture and its manifestations. Some may even say it is negative and does not paint culture in a positive light. From my experiences working with leaders, defining culture is not about positives or negatives—*culture just is*, and that is why it can be a challenge to describe it. Definitions of culture usually incorporate an expression of values and beliefs of groups, the learning that occurs in groups, and the expressions of those cultural norms.

The following is a definition of culture that is used in this book and that will be useful in your work:[3]

> Culture consists of the shared beliefs, values, and assumptions of a group of people who learn from one another and teach to others that their behaviors, attitudes, and perspectives are the correct ways to think, act, and feel.

It is helpful if you can think about culture in the following five ways:

- Culture is learned.
- Culture is shared.
- Culture is dynamic.

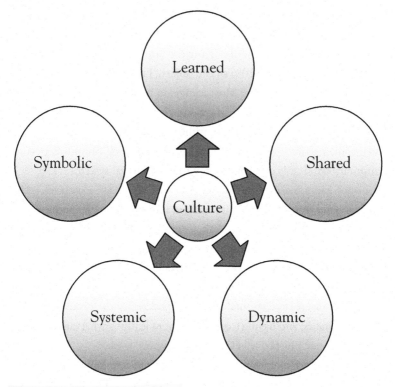

Figure 2.2. Elements of culture.

- Culture is systemic.
- Culture is symbolic.

Culture Is Learned

Geert Hofstede[4] views culture as consisting of mental programs, calling it *softwares of the mind,* meaning each person "carries within him or herself patterns of thinking, feeling, and potential acting which were learned throughout their lifetime."[5] Similarly, Peter Senge[6] argued that mental models lock individuals and groups into a specific perception about the world. Like a computer, we are programmed to act or behave in certain ways. The conscious and unconscious learning we undergo, over time, turns into beliefs that we consider to be valid. We then teach each other that these beliefs are cultural norms, and they are then expressed in our daily lives as behaviors and actions.

Think about your first day with your current organization or one you worked for in the past. Typically, your boss or a coworker gave you an orientation to the company, describing its mission, products, and services. Most likely, you met your coworkers and received a tour of the office facilities. Perhaps you met and talked with coworkers to get a sense of how your job related to their work. Maybe you spent time reading company materials, reviewing your department files, or talking with your supervisor about the details of your job responsibilities. Perhaps you had lunch with other staff members and were told about some parts of the organization such as, "Jane Doe should be fired but is still working here," "The CEO has control issues," or "The fax machine breaks down three times a day." Whatever you did in those first hours or days of orientation and training, you created an image of how you would fit into the company. In that moment, you told yourself a story of how you would work with the company and how it would work with you because others in that business culture told you how you needed to behave. This moment is so powerful that it shapes your experiences, including your thoughts, actions, behaviors, beliefs, and attitudes for the rest of your time with the company.

Culture Is Shared

Ming is a recent college graduate with a degree in accounting. She has taken a job with a large accounting firm. Although she gets along with members of her department and team, she tends to spend her free time with other colleagues who are of Asian descent, especially those who are in her generation. She feels that this group of coworkers understands her better and shares her values and ideas around work–life balance.

John has been with his state employer for 30 years, working up the ranks into seniority in his state agency. It's been customary for him and six coworkers of his age group to meet for lunch every day and discuss the latest sporting events. Once a week during the summer they meet up after work to play baseball at a local park and recreation site.

These two examples describe culture as a shared learning experience. Although you may think of yourself as an individual, you share beliefs, rituals, ceremonies, traditions, and assumptions with people who grew up or live in similar cultural backgrounds. It is easier for you to relate to someone who has shared value systems and ways of doing things than someone who does not share the same values.

The patterns of culture bind us together and enable us to get along with each other. Even though it feels good to be around people who think, act, and behave the same as you, shared learning can create blind spots. Shared cultures create a dynamic of an in-group, where people segregate themselves from each other. Within teams in organizations, in-group blind spots can lead to "group think," a termed coined by Irving Janis[7] to explain the ways in which groups ignore alternative solutions and take on actions and behaviors that discount the experiences for others.

Culture Is Dynamic

Culture is dynamic and thus complex. Culture is fluid rather than static, which means that culture changes all the time, every day, in subtle and tangible ways. Because humans communicate and express their cultural systems in a variety of ways, it can be hard to pinpoint exactly what cultural dynamics are at play. Consider, for example, a conversation about a person's attitude or feelings. In this type of conversation, Albert Meharbian[8] found that people pay attention to (a) the words, or what is being said; (b) the tone, or how the words are said; and (c) the visual behind the words, often called the body language. All of these are aspects of culture that are interpreted differently depending on the cultural context. Add multiple layers of culture to the conversation—such as time, power and authority, emotion, age, gender, religion, nationality, and even previous intercultural interactions—and communication at a cross-cultural level becomes complex and hard to manage. The following is an example of the dynamism of cultures:

> Shelia is the director of marketing for a social services agency. She provides feedback to one of her managers about how to improve services. Shelia sits behind a large executive desk and is leaning forward. The employee sits with her arms crossed, leaning away from Shelia.

If you were observing this scene, are you able to tell from the body language what each person is thinking? Why or why not? What cultural factors might be present?

In the example, Sheila's body language can be interpreted as any of the following: eager to assist or help, intensely interested in what the employee has to say, aggressive and wanting more information, or needing deeper engagement in the conversation. Her employee's body language could mean any of the following: protective, suspicious, not caring, or relaxed. To understand the dynamics of culture in this example, you would need to pay attention to the things you do not see such as:

- Is Sheila older or younger than her employee?
- What has been their working relationship?
- Does Sheila naturally lean forward when speaking with her employees?
- What is the tone of voice in the conversation?

Culture Is Systemic

In systems theory, systems are interrelated, interconnected parts that create a whole. There are patterns of behavior, deeply rooted structural systems, which are beneath the waterline. What we see at the top of the iceberg are the behaviors; we do not see what contributes to those behaviors. Consider, for example, a White woman walking down a quiet street. She quickly clutches her handbag closer to her body as she passes a Black man. Then, when she spots a White man walking toward her, she loosens her hold on the purse.

To address the system, one must be able to address the underlying patterns. These patterns, because they are deeply embedded in the system, will take up significant effort, time, and resources. Changes to the system are slow and gradual; visible changes may not appear until months, or even years, later.

Because most leaders spend their time evaluating and finding solutions to an "event," they revisit the issues over and over again, with no positive and sustainable results. The following case study illustrates the systemic nature of culture:

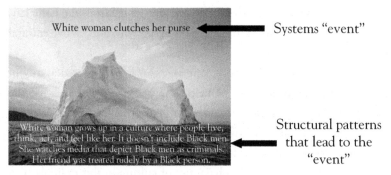

Figure 2.3. Culture from a systems approach.

Langley, Knox, and Cooper, a law firm in the Midwest, knows that it has to do more to be inclusive to women attorneys. It has met challenges in retaining its female workforce. The majority of women hired to work at the firm leave within a 3-year period. To address the issue, the firm provides gender sensitivity training to the entire company, attends graduate career fairs to actively recruit female attorneys, and has quotas for promoting women. However, the efforts in the past 5 years have yielded few results.

Langley, Knox, and Cooper focus much of their attention on the "events" of the system: women leaving after 3 years or providing gender sensitivity training. A look at the structural patterns reveals a more complex issue that cannot be solved through training and career fairs. The structural pattern is an insidious belief that women enter the law profession with the same opportunities and access to practicing law as men in the firm. Underlying this belief are more patterns of thought that keep this structural pattern in place. Possible patterns of thought could be:

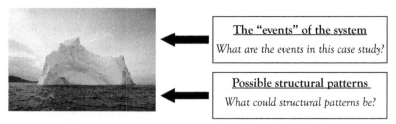

Figure 2.4. A systems approach to find structural patterns in gender conflicts.

- Other women attorneys don't have this problem, what's the big deal here?
- Everyone faces the same challenges in making partner. It's part of becoming a lawyer.
- We match our junior attorneys with senior attorneys who serve as their mentors. Everyone gets the same level of attention, so I am not sure what all the complaints are about.
- This law firm is different from others. If they don't like it here, then they can leave.
- We give the women in this firm more time off and flexibility than ever before, yet they still think it's not enough.

Understanding the thoughts help leaders to recognize that yearly gender sensitivity training would never work. These thought patterns, when combined and supported (intentionally or not), are difficult to unravel. The systemic nature of the problem becomes more complex and chaotic as time goes by and the issues are not addressed.

Culture Is Symbolic

Symbols are both verbal and nonverbal in form within cultural systems, and they have a unique way of linking human beings to each other. Humans create meaning between symbols and what they represent; as a result, different interpretations of a symbol can occur in different cultural contexts. Take, for example, a meeting of senior executives who need to make a decision about a new service. This group of leaders has a team culture that orients itself toward a democratic process: decision making is based on one vote from each member. Now imagine a similar group of leaders with the same task, but this time, the group of leaders comprises Native Americans. Leaders who are younger in the group ask their elders for advice. This is an example of how cultural systems differ in their interpretation and expressions of culture. In some cultural systems, voting is not an option. The symbol of a *vote* has different meanings and interpretations—or simply may not even exist in any practical sense—depending on the cultural background.

Stereotypes and Generalizations

One of the things that can happen in the context of discussing culture is falling into the stereotypes and generalizations of a cultural group or norm. It is important to recognize the difference and the impact these factors have in cultural interactions. In general, stereotypes are negative statements and interpretations made about a group of people. Stereotypes, whether deemed positive or negative, place people into boxes and categories and limit them to those specific perspectives. A stereotype, such as "Asians are good at math," does not provide the complete picture someone needs to understand the Asian culture or the differences between Asian cultures. Similarly, just because you meet a 70-year-old who does not know how to use current technology, it does not mean that other individuals in that generation do not know how to use it.

By contrast, generalizations of cultures are broad statements based on facts, experiences, examples, or logic. There are two kinds of generalizations, valid and faulty, and it is your role to determine which generalizations have validity behind them. Broad characterization of cultural groups can serve as a framework for cultural interactions. For example, Hispanic societies have a high degree of machismo, or in Middle Eastern cultures, women have a lesser status than men—these types of generalizations are helpful when engaging with people of those cultures. But in all cultural interactions, culturally intelligent leadership requires you to recognize that generalizations do not apply to everyone within a cultural group.

Levels of Culture

One of the basic tenets of culture is that it consists of levels and sublevels. It is useful to think about culture in terms of five basic levels: national, regional, organizational, team, and individual. Within each of these levels are tangible and intangible sublevels of culture.

National Culture

A businesswoman from the United States is in Germany for contract negotiations between her employer and a large German bank. The meeting is scheduled for nine o'clock in the morning. When she arrives to the meeting a few minutes before its start time, she is amazed that all her German counterparts are already seated and ready to begin the meeting. A few days later, upon her arrival back to the United States, she remarks to her American colleagues about her experience with German culture. In particular, she notes their level of attentiveness to punctuality and planning and says, "I thought we were punctual here in the United States! It's nothing compared to how Germans view punctuality."

This example illustrates the national differences between two cultures: American and German. National differences refer to the cultural influences of a nation that result in its national characteristics. Although nation-states have regional and political differences, national culture can be viewed as the values held by a majority of the population within the nation. These values are largely unconscious and developed throughout one's childhood. The values are pushed to a level of consciousness when in contrast to another nation's cultural values.

Within national cultures, values are generally seen as stable over time. National values, because they reflect the traditions of the nation-state over time, will change slightly from generation to generation, but the overall values will remain the same. For example, a German who comes from a culture of punctuality and travels for business in Italy will notice a national cultural difference in how Italians view time (more leisurely and relaxed) as compared to their own national culture.

Regional Culture

An interesting thing about living in the United States is the regional differences that make each part of the country unique. When I attended college in Boston, I heard the expression "wicked" used quite often. After asking my New England friends what "wicked" meant, I learned that it was used to emphasize a point. If I attended a concert that I really enjoyed, I would say, "That concert was awesome!" New Englanders would say, "That concert was wicked awesome." After living in the Boston area for 4 years, the word became a part of my vocabulary.

When I used the word in conversations with my friends and family members in Minnesota, they did not understand what I meant.

All national cultures consist of regional subcultures that influence the characteristics of one group from another in a nation state. The word "pop" refers to a soft drink in the Midwest, but if you go to the East Coast, it is referred to as "soda." In other regions of the United States, a soft drink is referred to as "Coke." The following is an example of regional cultural differences and one way the difference is expressed:

> Dianne moves from Texas for a job opportunity in Georgia. She lives in Georgia for 25 years and feels that it is her home state. However, her neighbors and coworkers do not think that she is a Georgian. Even though Dianne thinks she is from the south, she is reminded by others that she is "not a southerner."

Dianne experiences a regional cultural shift that she did not know existed until her move. Although she considers herself a Georgian, she is constantly reminded that she is not a southerner. At a conscious and unconscious level, her regional cultural experiences will dictate her thoughts about herself and others. She may develop the following assumptions and beliefs as a result of the regional cultural influences:

- I better just tell people that I am from Texas.
- Georgians think that you have to be from certain states to be considered a "southerner."
- If you are from the south, you must have lineage or roots that directly link you to the south. A "transplant" is not considered a true southerner.

What are regional differences and similarities that you have experienced or have been a part of? The following is a chart to help you identify regional similarities and cultures. In the column labeled "*Regional Culture Names*," write down two regions of a nation or country, such as West Coast and New England. Then, for each cultural expression listed, write down the regional similarities and differences you notice about each region you have chosen to identify.

Table 2.1. Exercise to Identify Regional Cultural Differences and Similarities

Regional Culture Names	Cultural Expression	Regional Differences	Regional Similarities
	Food		
	Dress code		
	Language		
	Housing		
	Music		

Organizational Culture

When you walk into a Target Store, what do you see? What does it look like? What kinds of items do they sell? What do you see when you walk into a Wal-Mart? What does it look like? What types of people shop at Wal-Mart? Who works there?

Shoppers have different experiences walking into a Target versus a Wal-Mart store because even though they are both retailers, their buildings are different, the types of products they carry vary from each other, the workers wear different clothes, the layout of a Wal-Mart store is very different from the layout of a Target store, and the behaviors expressed by workers in each organization are unique to each retailer. These elements give the organization its distinct culture that separates it from the other.

Organizational culture speaks to the culture that is specific to an organization—the culture that makes it distinctive from competitors and non-competitors. Organizational cultures are often referred to as "corporate cultures" and reflect the beliefs, values, and assumptions of an organization. For example, the culture of one school in a school district can be different than the culture of another school located in the same district simply because of what the people in one school's culture adhere and react to.

Team Culture

Lupe oversees a business division that includes sales people, engineers, researchers, and customer service staff. All teams work in different ways to accomplish their business strategies, but they also have work that is cross functional, relying on each other to get their work completed. At times, Lupe is overwhelmed at the teams' cultural differences and the impact it has on productivity and sales. She knows that each team has their own working styles, but she didn't realize how much these styles could interfere in the day-to-day operations of the division.

The sales department seems more outgoing and energetic than her engineers, who as a whole seem introverted and serious. Her researchers are detailed and scientific in nature, always questioning the tactics of the sales people. Her customer service employees are by nature people- and service-friendly and always wanting to make sure everyone gets along. These departments work well, but Lupe knows that silos in the organization can hinder growth and creativity.

The example above illustrates culture at the team level. The values, beliefs, and norms of culture are present in team environments, dictating the team's operations and efficiency. Cultural norms in teams guide members in their dress and appearance, their language, how they relate to one another, and how they get along. Some teams are very serious, while others use humor in their work life. Departments, teams, or workgroups can, and will, act very differently from each other even though they are located in the same building and in the same organization. Although you might not think about personality or temperament as cultural elements, they can and do shape a team's culture.

Individual Culture

Individual cultural differences relate to your preferences for things through your personal experiences that include the influence of your family, your peers, school, media, coworkers, and so on. You may share a national culture, such as being an American, with another person and live in the same regional culture, the Midwest. You may even work with the person in the same organization and department, thus sharing an organizational and team culture, and even though you share similar interests, you will likely have differences in individual culture based on who you are and your social upbringing. The following example illustrates these individual differences:

Bao, 31 years old, and Hua, 32 years old, are both Chinese American managers living in San Francisco. They both grew up in the area as third generation Chinese Americans. Both attended universities on the East Coast in the same city and majored in public policy. Bao and Hua work for a national nonprofit that funds grassroots leadership projects in Chinese-American communities in the United States. Both work in the programming department of their organization and have been there 4 years each.

Bao and Hua, although similar in their cultural backgrounds, have different perspectives based on their individual cultures. Bao's mother passed away while she was very young and she was raised by her father and aunts. Her father was not around because of long work hours. Bao, with the help of her aunts, raised her younger siblings. Her mother's death was a significant event in her life as she felt she did not have the mother-daughter relationship that many of her peers did. As a result she is overly protective.

Hua is the youngest child in her family. Both her parents are still alive. Hua was raised around many of her relatives who took care of her while her parents were working. She has always been given what she wanted or needed. Whenever Hua had a problem, her older siblings took care of the situation. As a result, Hua is quite relaxed in her demeanor and approach to life.

When Bao and Hua make programming decisions, Bao approaches her decision-making process from a methodical and careful perspective, always looking out for the program's and organization's needs. Hua, on the other side, is more relaxed in her approach, more willing to allow for flexibility and ambiguity.

Bao and Hua's cultural experiences have shaped them into different individuals and have impacted their managerial and leadership styles. Even though they share many similar cultural experiences, their individual cultural experiences have strong influences on them. Bao's methodical and careful decision-making processes are a result of her having to be responsible at a very early age. Hua's relaxed approach comes about because of her experiences as the youngest child and always knowing that she would be taken care of—that everything would be okay in the end.

These five levels of culture are important to think about and recognize, but it should also be understood that each of these cultures can be expressed in subcultures or microcultures. Not everyone acts or behaves the same in a national culture such as the United States. There are regional, county, and city differences within the national culture of being an "American." There are religious differences as well as gender cultures, ability and disability cultures, cultures revolving around sexual orientation, and even cultures centered around concepts or states of being, for example, the culture of homelessness or the culture of juvenile delinquency.

The Roots of Culture

Cultures show up in many forms and are expressed differently. Yet all forms and levels of cultures express and share three fundamental aspects: values, assumptions, and symbols.

Values

You need to recognize that value systems are fundamental to understanding how culture expresses itself. Values often serve as principles that guide people in their behaviors and actions. Our values, ideally, should match up with what we say we will do, and our values are most evident in symbolic forms. Consider, for example, a picture of the American flag. If you were an American, what words do the pictures evoke for you? *Freedom, liberty, America, united, independence, democracy,* or *patriotism,* perhaps?

What if a Nazi symbol were painted on the American flag? How would that make you feel? *Disgusted, sad, angry, revengeful?* What would the desecration of the flag symbolize? *Hatred, terrorism, nationalism?* What about *freedom of speech?* Symbols like the American flag evoke strong emotions for people, and when the symbol is desecrated, it can feel like a personal attack on the person's value system and their beliefs about the world. It feels out of alignment from what we believe to be true—what we see as our reality of the world. This is because our values and beliefs are rooted in stories we tell ourselves over and over again.

Joseph Campbell[9] noted that stories and myths are our psychological maps of the world. We use them to guide our thinking and behaviors, and when we do not like a story or it does not align with stories we know, we discard them. We learn through culture to create a story about the story. Campbell said that when we can unravel our stories, we begin to see the meaning we have placed on them and the impact they have on our lives. The case study that follows illustrates this notion of values:

> James works full time managing a fast food restaurant chain. Working extra hours every week helps him bring home more income for his family of four. He will do whatever it takes to help take care of his family. Ana is also a manager in the same restaurant. She works her 40 hours a week and then goes home to her family of three. She doesn't want to work more hours because she wants to spend as much time with her family as possible.

How does James's perspective of family differ from Ana's? What assumptions does each have about the value of *family*? What might be the stories they are creating for themselves that shape their values of family? Both individuals have the same value of *family*, but their values are expressed differently through their behaviors. A value such as family can be expressed and thought of differently from one culture to the next or from one person to the next. James believes that working hard illustrates his value of family, while Ana believes that spending time with her family demonstrates her commitment to the value. These assumptions are not expressed verbally, and, in some cases, the assumptions can be unconscious. Notice how, in the following scenario, James' assumptions are challenged:

> Both Ana and James receive a bonus for their work. James finds out that Ana has received the same percentage of bonus that he has. He's quite upset because he knows that he works more than she does and sometimes covers her shifts when she has family emergencies or is late because of day care issues. He thinks to himself, "How could she get the same bonus as me? She doesn't even work that hard, and she comes in late to her shift using excuses that her day care didn't show up again."

In the case study, the assumptions that James has of Ana (Ana makes excuses, Ana comes in late, or Ana does not work hard) can become a problem and conflict between the two. His assumptions are based on his own definition of family, which could consist of any of the following: be responsible, show up on time, or working hard can bring in more money for the family. His assumptions are challenged when Ana receives the same bonus for a perceived different level of commitment.

As a leader, it is important to understand and identify to employees that most of us share the same values. It is our interpretation and expression of the values that creates the conflict. Many people justify bias and discrimination on the grounds of "values" without realizing that it is not the values themselves but the difference between our expression and interpretation and that of those we come into conflict with.

Assumptions

Our values are supported by our assumptions of our world. They are beliefs or ideas that we believe and hold to be true. They come about through repetition. This repetition becomes a habit we form and leads to habitual patterns of thinking and doing. We do not realize our assumptions because they are ingrained in us at an unconscious level. We are aware of it when we encounter a value or belief that is different from ours, when it makes us feel that we need to stand up for, or validate, our beliefs.

In the iceberg analogy, assumptions are underneath the waterline. They define for us, and give life or meaning to, objects, people, places, and things in our lives. Our assumptions about our world determine how we react emotionally and what actions we need to take. The assumptions about our world views guide our behaviors and shape our attitudes. Consider, for example, the following case study:

> Kong grows up in SE Asia and has seen only males in leadership roles. Once he moves to the United States, he assumes males are the only authority figures. Meanwhile his daughters, Sheng and Lia, who have grown up in the United States and were raised with access to education and resources learn that they can be leaders. In their professional work they are seen by their peers as leaders.
>
> One day, at a celebration event that Sheng brings him to, Kong meets a White man who is her supervisor. He tells Kong,

"Your daughter is a great leader. She's really helped us through this transition." He replies politely, "Thank you." Later, Kong shares with his wife, Ka, the story. He says, "I don't know why he thinks Sheng is a leader. Women are not leaders. Only men are leaders."

Symbols

Anthropologist Clifford Geertz[10] believed that culture was a system based on symbols. He said that people use symbols to define their world and express their emotions. As human beings, we all learn, both consciously and unconsciously, starting at a very young age. What we internalize comes through observation, experience, interaction, and what we are taught. We manipulate symbols to create meaning and stories that dictate our behaviors, to organize our lives, and to interact with others. The meanings we attach to symbols are arbitrary. Looking someone in the eye means that you are direct and respectful in some countries, yet, in other cultural systems, looking away is a sign of respect. The meanings we attach to symbols can create a cultural havoc when we meet someone who believes in a different meaning or interpretation; it can give us culture shock. This shock can be disorientating, confusing, or surprising. It can bring on anxiety or nervousness and, for some a sense of losing control.

While training senior managers in a leadership program, the issue of the organization's dress code came up in our conversation about differences. All the managers were in agreement that there was a dress code problem. It seemed to the managers that a couple of the employees were not abiding by the dress code policy. At this midsize organization, the dress code was business casual, but a couple of the employees (the younger ones to be exact) came into work wearing t-shirts or dresses with thin straps. The managers were all confused as to why the dress code was so hard to follow for these two employees. It was obvious to them that business casual meant looking professional and neat, wearing clothes that were pressed and crisp. No matter how many times the dress code was explained to the staff, these two employees never changed.

In the training, we deconstructed the issue to understand what was really at play. The managers recognized that the dress code of "business casual" could mean several things if not explicitly stated in the policy. In fact, one manager said, "We keep saying that business casual is common sense, but our idea of common sense could be completely different from that employee's version of common sense." They also discovered that they did not want to be so explicit as to name every article of clothing that employees could and could not wear. They felt that being explicit would take away the feeling or the symbol that the office was a casual and relaxed environment; having policies that dictated everything that someone could or could not do would symbolize a different type of working environment.

As a result of this conversation, the managers recognized the tangible ways in which symbols are manifested in organizations. They became more mindful of the language and words used. They were more intentional about their behavior, now recognizing that each of their reactions or nonreactions is a symbol.

Value Dimensions of Culture

The work of Geert Hofstede,[11] while employed at IBM in the late 1960s to early 1970s, still stands as one of the most comprehensive studies of cultural values on leadership in the workplace. From his data collected from over 30 countries and 100,000 individuals, Hofstede created a model of value dimensions that speak to the ways that cultures tend to operate. Although this study is generalized to specific countries, his work on cultural value dimensions is helpful to any business doing global and multicultural work.

According to Hofstede, the five main dimensions are *identity*, *power*, *gender*, *uncertainty*, and *time*. You can think about cultural value dimensions on a scale or a continuum, where one aspect of the value lies on one side of the scale and the other extreme lies at the other end of the scale.

Table 2.2. Five Cultural Value Dimensions

Value Dimensions	One Extreme	Other Extreme
Identity	Group	Individual
Power	Egalitarian	Hierarchal
Gender	Feminine	Masculine
Uncertainty	Ambiguity	Structure
Time	Relationship	Task

Cultural value dimensions help you to understand culture and to be able to make sense of culture. These dimensions provide you with a perspective of culture for yourself as well as a perspective of how others perceive their culture. All cultures experience these dimensions of difference in many ways, and different cultures solve these differences in many ways. Becoming aware of these concepts helps you to figure out the experiences you have in relation to your culture. It helps to make that experience less ambiguous and threatening. Cultural value dimensions provide clarity and a starting place for cultural awareness. However, they are often seen as intangible and under the waterline, but once you adapt to the cultural dimensions, you become more comfortable and do not see the cultural difference.

Identity

The value dimension of *identity* refers to the attention of groups or individuals toward group needs versus individual needs as well as toward individual achievement and interpersonal relationships. On a continuum, you see the identity value dimension expressed as such in Figure 2.5.

On one spectrum, there is an expectation of doing things for the group rather than for oneself. On the other side, achievements and needs are individualized. Hofstede[12] found that cultures placing a high value on individualism and a low value on collectivism valued individual rights; cultures placing a high value on collectivism valued relationships and harmony. This orientation, he argued, can have a large affect on managing organizations and people.

For example, in many Latino cultures, the concept of family, *la familia*, is critical to their cultural history and social systems. *La familia* is the most important social unit and includes extended family members.

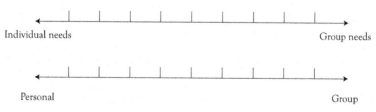

Figure 2.5. Dimension of identity.

Decision making, conflict resolution, and negotiation are based on group needs rather than individual preferences; through paying attention to group and collective needs, harmony and relationships are intact. Alternatively, in individualistic cultures, the need of the individual comes first. U.S. culture teaches this to children at a young age. The following is an example that illustrates the differences between individualist and collectivist cultures:

> Mary takes her 8-year-old, Johnny, to the store to buy ice cream. She asks him to choose what ice-cream flavor he would like. Over time he learns to tell his mother about his personal likes and dislikes. Every time his mother responds to his decisions with encouragement. Over time he learns that he can and should be able to express himself.

By encouraging her child to make decisions and choices on his own, Mary raises a child that considers his personal needs and wants. If Johnny was in a group that operated more collectively, he might become quite upset when told that the whole group must agree to a specific ice cream flavor, that is, that his personal choice does not matter in the group decision.

The following is another example of individual and collective cultures:

> A history teacher gives a lesson on the Bill of Rights to her students. She explains that everyone has individual rights and liberties. Sahara is a student in the class. She is 13 years old and a recent immigrant from Somalia. She learns that she has individual rights and to the disappointment and frustration of her parents, her behaviors begin to change at home. She comes home late from school, she stops doing her chores, and she talks back to her mother. She says, "I can do whatever I want. In this country, I am free!"

Sahara comes from a culture that is collective and tribal in nature. Her parents express confusion when they hear her say, "I can do whatever I want." They do not understand what she means and why she says what she says. They begin to think that she is losing her cultural values.

The following is another example that illustrates the value differences between collectivist and individualist cultures:

> Tabitha is 22 years old and moves in with her college boyfriend, Randy, to an apartment near her parents. Tom and Susan, Tabitha's parents, are excited that she is able to be independent and to live on her own.
>
> Xioli is Tabitha and Randy's friend from college. She is Chinese American and wants to move out of her parents' house. Randy and Tabitha have offered the second bedroom space for Xioli in their apartment. Xioli's parents think she is too young to live on her own. They also think it is a sign of disrespect to them if she, as a single woman, lives with a man.

Power

Hofstede defined power distance dimensions as maintaining strict rules that establish the types of relationships individuals have with one another. Power represents the level of inequality and equality, as well as the level of hierarchy and upward mobility, within a cultural group. In regard to leadership, power dimension can also represent a culture's tendencies toward authority, on one end, and one's orientation toward laissez-faire leadership, on the other. Hofstede found that low-power-distance cultures emphasized equality and minimized power and status. The following is an example of this:

> Susan is the president of a large manufacturing business. Although she is in a position of leadership and authority, she takes a "hands off management approach" to her employees and in meetings provides a participatory, democratic engagement process.

Susan's dimension of power is illustrated in Figure 2.6.

Gender

Hofstede[13] describes the value dimension of gender as representing two paradigms of thinking and practice about the world in relation to

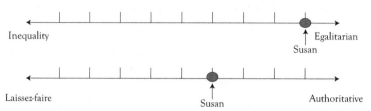

Figure 2.6. Power value dimension.

traditional values associated with gender roles. Gender refers to the culture's tendencies or orientation toward enforcing or reinforcing masculine and feminine roles in work. Masculine cultures tend to emphasize ambition, control, competition, assertiveness, and achievement, whereas feminine cultures emphasize nurture, care, sharing, quality of life, and relationships. Sometimes these values are expressed as the "quantity of life" and the "quality of life."

In his findings, Hofstede indicated that cultures that rate high in masculinity, such as Japan, Austria, Venezuela, and Italy, revealed a high proportion of males in dominant structures; in low masculine cultures, such as Denmark, Norway, Netherlands, and Sweden, women were treated more equally in their social systems.

It is important that you recognize that these values are not associated with being male or female. In other words, this does not mean that men cannot be part of feminine cultures or that women do not orient themselves toward "masculine" cultural values. Finally, like other value dimensions, gender dimensions can vary greatly within any culture.

You can think about the value dimension of gender in the ways displayed in Figure 2.7.

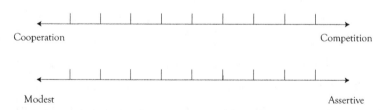

Figure 2.7. Gender dimensions.

Uncertainty

The dimension of uncertainty emphasizes cultures that are either oriented toward uncertainty or toward creating certainty and stability. Hofstede described this as a society's tolerance for ambiguity.[14] Societies that are in *high uncertainty avoidance* are rule-bound and pay more attention to written procedures, rules, or goals. Individuals who have a higher need for formalized structures, procedures, or diplomacy tend to minimize their uncertainty levels in order to cope with the unknowns of their situations. Someone who is on the other extreme of the dimension is more relaxed about the rules and procedures; they are more flexible in their attitudes toward rules and policies. The value dimension can be expressed in the ways shown in Figure 2.8.

This dimension also speaks to a culture's orientation toward directness and honesty. Edward Hall[15] popularized the terms "high-text" culture and "low-text" culture to describe cultural differences between two different types of societies. The ideas are often used to describe the ways in which cultures communicate and to understand what cultural constructs underlie the communication.

High-context cultures are societies in which people often make inferences; they leave things unsaid, knowing that the other person would understand what was implied in the communication. People in these societies tend to rely on groups for support. Low-context cultures are societies that are explicit and direct in their communication. They generally are more comfortable relying on themselves, as individuals, and working out solutions to problems. Like high-context cultures, relationships are important to low-context societies; the difference is in the longevity of the relationships. Generally, low-context societies have many relationships that are less intimate and close than those of high-context cultures.

Both types of cultural differentiations are illustrated in Table 2.3.

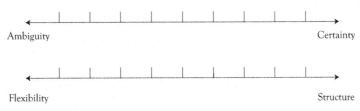

Figure 2.8. Uncertainty value dimension.

Table 2.3. High and Low Context Culture Descriptors

Cultural Context	Countries/ Cultures	Descriptors	How They Perceive the Other Context
High context	Spain Mexico Greece Middle East China Japan Korean Thailand	• Less verbally explicit communication • Implied meanings • Long-term relationships • Decisions and activities focus around personal, face-to-face relationships	Low-context cultures are . . . • relationship-avoidant • too aggressive • focused too much on tasks and goals
Low context	United States Germany Great Britain Australia	• Rule-oriented • Knowledge is public and accessible • Short-term relationships • Task-centered	High-context cultures . . . • are too ambiguous • are quiet and modest • ask a lot of questions

Time

The dimension of time speaks to how communities are oriented toward space and time, including their tendencies toward traditions and the past and their orientation toward the future and the present. In many cultural systems, holding on to traditions is important in current day-to-day operations and relationships. Some societies will refer to traditions to preserve and maintain cultural norms, that is, to protect what currently exists.

Time is also a reference to a culture's orientation toward tasks or relationships. For example, a manager from the United States who travels to India to negotiate a business contract needs to know that meetings will occur whenever people show up to the meeting, which could be hours after it is scheduled. A task-oriented leader is certain to be frustrated when he meets up with an Indian who is more time-oriented toward relationships. In the American perspective, promptness is professionalism; yet, in the other perspective, the concept of time is more loose and flexible. The value of time is illustrated in Figure 2.9.

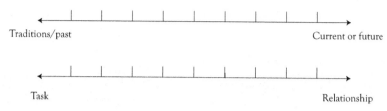

Traditions/past   Current or future

Task   Relationship

Figure 2.9. Time value dimension.

Understanding these five value dimensions and their impact in different cultural systems will be helpful to your work in cultural intelligence. Like any cultural model, you need to recognize that cultural factors in leadership and organizations, as indicated by Taylor Cox, differ "across gender, nationality, and racial/ethnic groups as it relates to time and space orientation, leadership style orientations, individualism versus collectivism, competitive versus cooperative behavior, locus of control, and communication styles."[16] You must recognize that *microcultures* exist within *macrocultures*; this is significant in working effectively on a cross-cultural level.[17]

Culture and Leadership

What is the importance of understanding cultural value dimensions in businesses? Like other cultural systems, organizational culture controls the behavior, values, assumptions, and beliefs of organizational members. It is a combination of organizational members' *own* beliefs and the values, beliefs, and assumptions of the organization. It is the role of the organizational leader, as a change agent, to help create a positive organizational culture that meets the demands of a competitive environment, board and shareholder expectations, and employee career satisfaction.

Since the mid-1990s, the Global Leadership and Organizational Behavior Effectiveness (GLOBE)[18] research of 62 societies has served as a significant study for understanding how cultural value dimensions are expressed in different cultures—whether societal or organizational. Knowledge and awareness of cultural values can enable leaders and managers to effectively manage and work through intercultural conflict and interactions. Over 17,000 managers from 951 organizations in 62 societies participated in focus groups, questionnaires, and interviews for this study.

Cultural Value Dimensions

The GLOBE study found that nine core dimensions of cultures exist in different societies. The first six dimensions in Table 2.4 originated from the cultural value dimensions Geert Hofstede proposed in the 1980s. Table 2.4 lists other dimensions, as well as their definitions, as described in the GLOBE study.[19]

Based on the responses generated by the study and using other research, the GLOBE researchers grouped societies into regional clusters. The clusters were a way of creating meaning around societal views of culture and leadership. Each cluster had characteristics specific to their region, language, religion, history, and shared cultural understanding. Tables 2.5 and 2.6 list each cluster and the countries that were grouped into the clusters.

Leadership Behaviors and Culture

The findings of the GLOBE study served to help organizations and societies understand what made an effective or ineffective leader. Many leadership behaviors are similar across societies, pointing out that no matter the cultural difference or society in which a leader is from, there are specific leadership behaviors that are viewed as effective. The GLOBE project was significant in indicating how cultures perceive effective and ineffective leadership, which is helpful to leaders in facilitating intercultural interactions.

The study revealed six global leadership behaviors, which were used in the study to understand how the clusters perceived leadership. These six are charismatic/value-based, team-oriented, participative, humane-oriented, autonomous, and self-protective. Using their understanding of leadership behaviors and perceptions of leadership from each cluster group, the researchers were able to identify a leadership profile for each cluster. Tables 2.7 and 2.8 list the six leadership

Table 2.4. Cultural Dimensions as Researched in the GLOBE Study

Globe Dimension	One Extreme	Other Extreme
Uncertainty avoidance	Need for established social norms, rituals, and practices	Comfortable with ambiguity and predictability
Power distance	Egalitarian and nonhierarchal	Hierarchy, authority, disparity in status and wealth
Institutional collectivism	Collective actions and sharing of resources encouraged	Individual actions and goals are encouraged
In-group collectivism	Expressions of pride, loyalty, and cohesion	Noncohesiveness, loyal to oneself and one's needs
Gender egalitarianism	Nurture, care, relationships, sharing	Ambition, assertiveness, control
Assertiveness	Assertive, confrontational, and aggressive in social relationships	Timid, submissive, and tender in social relationships
Future orientation	Planning, investing, and delays of individual or collective gratification	Spontaneity, enjoying the present
Performance orientation	Encourages and rewards group performance and excellence	No rewards and encouragement for goals; more relaxed in terms of achievement
Humane orientation	Encourages and rewards individuals for being fair, altruistic, friendly, generous, caring	Concerns for self, not sensitive, not encouraging of social supports and community values

Adapted from House et al. (2002) The GLOBE Study of 62 Societies, Thousand Oaks, CA: Sage.

behaviors and their characteristics as well as the leadership profile for each cluster.

The study also highlighted the perceptions of cultures related to universally desirable and undesirable attributes in leaders. The desirable attributes were viewed as characteristics that were valued and that facilitated the leadership processes. Undesirable attributes were viewed as obstacles and challenges to effective leadership. Table 2.9 illustrates the positive and negative attributes of effective leadership.

Table 2.5. GLOBE Clusters of Societies

Cluster	Countries
Anglo	Canada, United States, Australia, Ireland, England, South Africa (White sample), New Zealand
Confucian Asia	Singapore, Hong Kong, Taiwan, China, South Korea, Japan
Eastern Europe	Greece, Hungary, Albania, Slovenia, Poland, Russia, Georgia, Kazakhstan
Germanic Europe	Austria, The Netherlands, Switzerland, Germany-East, Germany-West
Latin America	Ecuador, El Salvador, Colombia, Bolivia, Brazil, Guatemala, Argentina, Costa Rica, Venezuela, Mexico
Latin Europe	Israel, Italy, Switzerland (French-speaking), Spain, Portugal, France
Middle East	Turkey, Kuwait, Egypt, Morocco, Qatar
Nordic Europe	Denmark, Finland, Sweden
Southern Asia	Philippines, Indonesia, Malaysia, India, Thailand, Iran
Sub-Saharan Africa	Zimbabwe, Namibia, Zambia, Nigeria, South Africa (Black sample)

Adapted from House et al. (2002) The GLOBE Study of 62 Societies, Thousand Oaks, CA: Sage

Table 2.6. Clusters of Societies and their Cultural Value Dimensions

Cultural Dimension	High-Score Cluster	Low-Score Cluster
Uncertainty avoidance	Germanic Europe Nordic Europe	Eastern Europe, Latin America Middle East
Power/hierarchy	No Clusters	Nordic Europe
Institutional collectivism	Nordic Europe Confucian Asia	Germanic Europe, Latin America Latin Europe
In-Group collectivism	Confucian Asian, Eastern Europe Latin America, Middle East Southern Asia	Anglo, Germanic Europe Nordic Europe
Gender	Eastern Europe Nordic Europe	Middle East

Adapted from House et al. (2002) The GLOBE Study of 62 Societies, Thousand Oaks, CA: Sage

Table 2.7. GLOBE Study of Key Leadership Behaviors

Dimension	Behaviors
Charismatic/value-based leadership	Inspires others, motivates, expect high performance; visionary, self-sacrificing, trustworthy, decisive
Team-oriented leadership	Team-building, common purpose, collaborative, integrative, diplomatic, not malevolent
Participative leadership	Participative and not autocratic; inclusive of others
Humane-oriented leadership	Supportive, considerate, compassionate and generous; modesty and sensitivity
Autonomous leadership	Independent and individualistic; autonomous and unique
Self-protective leadership	Ensures the safety and security of the leader and the group; self-centered, status conscious, face-saving, conflict-inducing

Adapted from House et al. (2002) The GLOBE Study of 62 Societies, Thousand Oaks, CA: Sage

Business leaders have tremendous power to change the organizational culture by utilizing several methods that address the underlying assumptions, beliefs, and values of its members; however, this is not an easy task. Culture, as explained, is oftentimes manifest in unconscious behaviors, values, and assumptions that develop over time and change as new employees enter an organization. The significance of the GLOBE study is that it helps leaders to understand the role of culture in leadership. By understanding one's culture, as well as that of others, it brings you to awareness of different perceptions of leadership and how cultures come to understand leaders. Recognizing the elements in leadership and culture enables you to leverage the differences that cultures create and to use that to create positive intercultural growth.

Chapter Summary

- Culture is comprised of both tangible and intangible things you see, hear, feel, and perceive. It consists of the shared beliefs, values, and assumptions of a group of people who learn from one another and teach to others that their behaviors, attitudes, and perspectives are the correct ways to think, act, and feel.
- Culture is a process of learning and sharing, and it is dynamic and symbolic.

Table 2.8. Leadership Behavior Profiles for Clusters

Cluster	1st	2nd	3rd	4th	5th	6th
Eastern Europe	Autonomous	Self-protective	Charismatic	Team Oriented	Humane	Participative
Latin America	Charismatic	Team	Self-protective	Participative	Humane	Autonomous
Latin Europe	Charismatic	Team	Participative	Self-protective	Humane	Autonomous
Confucian Asia	Self-protective	Team	Humane	Charismatic	Autonomous	Participative
Nordic Europe	Charismatic	Participative	Team	Autonomous	Humane	Self-protective
Anglo	Charismatic	Participative	Humane	Team	Autonomous	Self-protective
Sub-Sahara Africa	Humane	Charismatic	Team	Participative	Self-protective	Autonomous
Southern Asia	Self-protective	Charismatic	Humane	Team	Autonomous	Participative
Germanic Europe	Autonomous	Charismatic	Participative	Humane	Team	Self-protective
Middle East	Self-protective	Humane	Autonomous	Charismatic	Team	Participative

Adapted from House et al. (2002) The GLOBE Study of 62 Societies, Thousand Oaks, CA: Sage

Table 2.9. List of Desirable and Undesirable Leadership Attributes From the GLOBE Research

Desirable Leadership Attributes	Undesirable Leadership Attributes
Trustworthy	Loner
Just	Asocial
Honest	Noncooperative
Foresight	Irritable
Plans ahead	Nonexplicit
Encouraging	Egocentric
Positive	Ruthless
Dynamic	Dictatorial
Motivational	
Builds confidence	
Intelligent	
Dependable	
Team builder	
Communicator	

Adapted from House et al. (2002) The GLOBE Study of 62 Societies, Thousand Oaks, CA: Sage

- Cultural issues are systemic and understanding this helps leaders to appreciate culture in its fullest sense.
- Awareness helps to eliminate the stereotypes that are derived from cultural misunderstandings, which limit the positive ways in which culture is viewed. However, generalizations about cultures can help serve as a framework for interacting with unfamiliar cultural systems.
- Culture is multidimensional, consisting of multiple layers. There are five main levels—national, regional, organizational, team, and individual—that are most useful in cultural contexts.
- Each cultural layer, when peeled apart, reveals the "roots" of culture, which consist of the values, assumptions, and symbols of the culture. These three ground cultural systems, often making it hard for cultural shifts to occur.
- Familiarity with Hofstede's model of value dimensions (identity, power, gender, uncertainty, and time) in the workplace helps leaders to realize the impact of values and beliefs in cultural settings.

- The GLOBE study of 62 societies is the most comprehensive research, to date, that analyzes how leadership is perceived by cultures.
- Nine cultural value dimensions, including the five proposed by Hofstede in the 1980s, illustrate the importance of understanding value dimensions in the context of leading.
- There are six global leadership categories that emerged from the GLOBE data: charismatic, team-oriented, participative, humane-oriented, autonomous, and self-protective.
- The GLOBE data points to universally positive and undesirable attributes of leaders. All cultures agree that the following are negative attributes: a leader who is a loner, irritable, ruthless, asocial, nonexplicit, dictatorial, noncooperative, and egocentric.
- Leaders have a role in creating business cultures that make employees feel valued and included regardless of their cultural backgrounds.

CHAPTER 3

Cultural Intelligence Defined

A few years ago I was invited to speak about cultural intelligence at a global women's leadership conference in the United Arab Emirates. Like any country I am traveling to, I made the efforts to learn about the area of the world that I was going to visit. To prepare for my trip I found books that spoke about the cultural history and background of the country. I bought language CDs and watched documentaries about that region of the world. I also visited websites and blogs to explore what other travelers had done and experienced. I know I spent hours finding information and learning about the culture and the people, including what gestures to use and how to address someone in a business meeting—all the etiquettes I thought I would need in the country.

As a petite-sized woman traveling alone, late at night in an unfamiliar country, I was anxious to get to my hotel as soon as possible. Upon my arrival in the United Arab Emirates, I went through passport control like every passenger. When it was my turn, I handed my passport and plane ticket to the man behind the counter. He nodded at me and I responded with an enthusiastic "Hello." Then, the man looked at me for a few seconds and then looked away. In the seconds that he looked away, I looked toward the direction he was facing. I was not sure what drew his attention away, but his attention never came back to me and my passport.

I did not know what to do. Several thoughts were going through my head at that time. Perhaps I was in the wrong line? Did I do something wrong? Why is he not taking my passport? Was I supposed to get another form of documentation? Could something happen to me? Would I be able to call my peers at their hotel to let them know I arrived? Would someone be willing to come and pick me up?

I was the last person in my line going through passport control, and every line other than my own seemed to be moving. As I watched traveler after traveler go through passport control, I remember feeling very self-conscious and a bit worried. As I watched his attention focused on something else, I tried to draw it back by saying, "Hi!" hoping I would have his attention this time. No luck.

I felt my anxiety rising, mostly because of the worse-case scenario thinking I was doing. I kept telling myself "everything is going to be okay" although I had no idea if it was. I was not clear why the man in front of me was not taking my passport. I looked around for the non-verbal cues, but all I could tell was that he was acting as if he did not see me. Then, I thought I would check to see if there was something wrong with my passport, and I proceeded to say, "Is anything wrong?" No response.

I nudged the passport forward, and he turned his attention back on me. He still did not pick up the passport or acknowledge me. I began to shift the backpack I was carrying on my right shoulder to move the weight off, and then it dawned on me that maybe I should pass the passport to him with my right hand. I had read in the literature and online that in the Arab world, the left hand is considered unclean. Did I hand him the passport with my left hand? I may have since my right hand was grabbing the handles of my backpack.

I nudged the passport with my right hand toward him.

The Emirati responded by taking the passport! He stamped it and then said, "Have a good stay in our country."

When I reached my hotel, I could not go to sleep. My mind was replaying the scenario of the Emirati man and myself. How did I know what to do? What if I nudged the passport with my right hand and he still did not take it? What emotions were coming up for me? What more could I have done to understand the situation? Was this really a part of Muslim culture I was experiencing or was it the Emirati man's individual preferences and culture?

I will never forget this experience because it was my own cultural intelligence in action. I was trying to be culturally intelligent without having all the information and knowing only the details that were in front of me. The frustration of not knowing if what I said or did was offensive bothered me because I see myself as adaptable and respectful. And perhaps the man's reaction had nothing to do with me and all to do with how he was feeling in that moment. Although I sought to learn different parts about the culture before traveling to the Emirates, I gained from this experience the knowledge that one can never be prepared for what cultural interactions could bring in any given moment. This is why cultural intelligence (CI) is incredibly vital and useful as a tool; it is there to help you understand each play-by-play action in cultural interactions. CI helps you to break down your cognitive, emotional, and physical reactions, helping you to understand more about yourself so that in future interactions, you make different choices in how you react.

What Is Cultural Intelligence?

At the core of it, cultural intelligence is your ability to successfully adapt to unfamiliar cultural settings. Peter Earley and Elaine Mosakowski defined cultural intelligence as the ability to "tease out of a person's or group's behavior those features that would be true of all people and all groups, those peculiar to this person or this group, and those that are neither universal nor idiosyncratic."[1] Earley et al. wrote that cultural intelligence is not just about learning new cultural situations; it is creating "a new framework for understanding what he or she experiences and sees."[2] Similarly, David Thomas and Kerr Inkson indicated that cultural intelligence is about

> being skilled and flexible about understanding a culture, learning more about it from your on-going interactions with it, and gradually reshaping your thinking to be more sympathetic to the culture and your behaviors to be more skilled and appropriate when interacting with others from the culture.[3]

The idea of cultural intelligence is an immensely useful tool in business. It helps to bring attention to the differences in thought and behaviors due to cultural factors. Consistently practicing cultural intelligence has been known to increase the success of multicultural team performance. Leaders who are culturally intelligent have awareness of how culture contributes to communication and creates shared learning.[4]

Tuning Into Cultural Intelligence

On a business trip to Texas, my colleague, who had never visited the state, was surprised at the amount of "Spanish music" on the radio. Every time she found a music station or station providing information, the speakers and singers spoke in Spanish. She said, "I can't find any music that I can understand," and quickly changed to a local station that played top 40 and pop music.

When I suggested that we should try listening to different music and experience the cultural shift between our state and another, she said, "No way. I can't understand what they're saying!" I replied, "I can't either, but it's a part of the culture here and wouldn't it be interesting to be like one of the locals?" Her response, "That's okay. I'll just stick to what I know."

Cultural intelligence is like tuning into different stations, being able to adapt to one's new environment, and, in this case, tuning into the style of music in this region of the United States. Like my colleague, we all have particular stations that we like. Music that is familiar provides us with comfort. Tuning in to the same stations over and over again breeds familiarity with the songs and the types of programming broadcast by the stations. We even program the stations into our car radio so as to know exactly what buttons to push if we want to hear a specific music genre.

When you are in a different city or state, you begin to lose the signals of your favorite stations. Try as you might, the stations often do not come through. What might you do? You could find another station in that state that offers the same music or information that you like. Upon finding it, you might program it so as to not lose the station. However, what if the radio frequencies you encounter pick up limited stations? Like my colleague, you might turn off the radio or change the station back to one that is familiar. Or, like her, you could bring your own MP3 player with your own music.

Similarly, when you are in unfamiliar cultural settings, you realize that the signals you are receiving are vastly different from your own. You are not familiar with what your new surroundings are communicating to you. Your first reaction is to find something familiar, and you look for cues and signs to help you adjust. However, you cannot always rely on what you know and what you can bring with you. Like my coworker, bringing equipment, like an MP3 player, does not always guarantee successful integration. After many tries, she found out her MP3 player did not work in the rental car; she opted for turning off the radio altogether. In intercultural interactions, the equipment—that is, our skill sets and our knowledge—may not be enough to cope in a new cultural environment.

We need to be able to learn how to turn off or reset ourselves to better adapt to the new situation.

Cultural Intelligence Model

Cultural intelligence is a framework to help you learn to turn off your "cruise control." Like a computer that has been on too long, is working too hard, or has too many programs running that cause it to freeze, we have to learn to reset our mental programming. Sometimes, resetting it once or twice does not work; you will need to turn it off completely by taking a pause and then returning to it at a later time.

Cultural intelligence emphasizes three areas: metacognition and cognition, motivation, and behavior. Metacognition and cognition represent your ability to think, learn, and strategize. In CI, the principle of motivation refers to your self-efficacy and confidence, your ability to be persistent, and the alignment to your personal values. Behavior, in CI, is about your ability to have a repertoire of skills and your ability to adapt your behavior.

The framework for cultural intelligence consists of the following parts: knowledge, strategic thinking, motivation, and behaviors. It

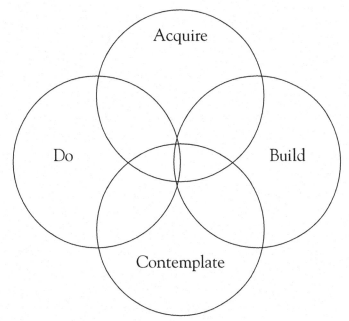

Figure 3.1. Cultural intelligence model.

may be helpful to think about these as the ABCs of CI: **A**cquire, **B**uild, **C**ontemplate, and **D**o. Each CI Principle is explored in the upcoming chapters,and more in-depth analysis of the tool occurs in Chapter 7.

Acquire Knowledge

A fundamental piece of inter- and cross-cultural interactions is the knowledge a leader has when working with cultures unfamiliar and different from his or her own. Knowledge is a central tenet in intercultural training and is included in the cultural intelligence model because it is essential for any person, whether leading or managing, to be attentive to cultural systems. You must know how cultures are created, interpreted, and shared, as well as how cultural interpretations, meaning, and symbols can impact behaviors and attitudes.

You can think about this aspect of the model as *acquire*, because you need to acquire information and knowledge that help you to identify cultural elements at play. The acquisition of knowledge—tapping into what you have stored in your memory—is cognition.

Build Your Strategic Thinking

Once you gain knowledge about the culture, how will you use it? What parts of the knowledge obtained will you use? Will they all fit, given the cultural setting? These questions address the component of cultural intelligence that speaks to your ability, as a leader, to strategize across cultures. It is your ability to *build* awareness of your surrounding through preparation and planning. It is often referred to as "metacognition."

Earley et al. noted, "Figuring out how things operate and what is appropriate in a new culture is detective work using the facts of the case—assemble them, order and organize them, interpret them, act on them."[5] Strategic thinking is important because it is how you think about, or make sense of, the knowledge and use it in a way that helps you better perform and interact with different cultures. If you are able to understand how you learn the information and how you have processed it, this helps you to make sense of unfamiliar situations. Early and Peterson[6] wrote that when there is a focus on metacognition, this component of CI can help people to develop and expand their behavioral repertoires.

Contemplate Your Motivation and Ability to Work With Others

The third element of the cultural intelligence model speaks to your ability to pay attention to your surroundings as well as your responses to unfamiliar situations. It is about reflecting upon your own interests, your drive, and your motivation, as well as your willingness to work through, and with, cultural interactions.

You can think about this component of the model as *contemplate* because it requires you to be present—to take a step back, suspend your judgments and biases, reflect upon your assumptions, and listen carefully. It requires that you be alert and remain aware of your cultural surroundings. As a leader, presence allows you to identify the cultural scripts that are hidden and to recognize when to turn them off.

Do Adapt and Perform

Richard Carlson said that "everything we do has the potential to influence another human being. . . . the key element here is not to second-guess yourself but rather to become conscious of how your life choices influence those around you."[7] Carlson speaks to our level of conscious choice in day-to-day living. When do we choose to adapt to our environments? Because of a choice we made, what did we let go? How has our choice affected our beliefs and values?

These questions address the fourth component of cultural intelligence, which is your adaptability and ability to perform new behaviors based on new cultural surroundings. Are you aware of how others see you and how you come across to them? How do you interpret what others say, and how do you respond? Culturally intelligent leaders are like chameleons in social environments, changing their behaviors to mimic their surroundings.

What Makes Cultural Intelligence Unique?

Howard Gardner[8] popularized the idea that intelligence is more than cognitive capacity—that human potential cannot be limited to cognitive intelligence the way it is described and defined in society. You can think about cultural intelligence as another form of intelligence. People with this particular intelligence have the ability to steer their way through unfamiliar cultural interactions; they do this in what seems to others as an effortless manner. This does not mean that culturally intelligent people are more intelligent overall than others; rather, those who are not skilled in this intelligence may need to adopt a different approach toward learning and improving their cultural intelligence.

According to Earley and Peterson, cultural intelligence is a significant improvement over existing approaches because it "provides an integrated approach to training dealing with knowledge and learning, motivation and behavior, and is built upon a unifying psychological model of cultural adaptation rather than the piecemeal and country-specific approach in training."[9] David Thomas and Kerr Inkson[10] wrote that, compared to emotional and social intelligence, cultural intelligence theory includes the influence of cultural factors and their impact in intercultural interactions.

Emotional intelligence is one's ability and capacity to identify, assess, and manage one's emotions as well as others' emotions. Although extremely important, emotional intelligence "presumes a degree of familiarity within a culture and context that may exist across many cultures for a given individual."[11] Similarly, the social cues picked up and used by someone with high social intelligence—that is, the ability and capacity to sense one's inner state, feelings, and thoughts in relation to one's social environment and react appropriately in this environment for social success[12]—differs from culture to culture.

Earley and Peterson argue that adaptation is a requirement when one enters new cultural contexts, and cultural intelligence provides the theoretical background for understanding how one would need to adjust, adapt, or reinvent oneself based on the culture and the situation.[13] Someone with high emotional and social intelligence is not guaranteed to be culturally intelligent, although having those skills can make it easier for them to learn about cultural intelligence. This is illustrated in the following case study.

Martha works as a program director for a large nonprofit that directs volunteer programs. Her coworkers describe her as, "personable, outgoing, empathic, and caring." Whenever there is conflict or unsettled business, she is the "go-to person" for helping her colleagues work out their issues. Her ability to be empathetic enables her to understand others' thoughts and feelings as well as their intentions.

When Martha gets upset or frustrated, she "takes a pause" or will back away from the issue or person until she can get a hold of her emotions. If Martha is asked how she manages her emotions, she replies that meditation and exercise help her to regulate how she feels from moment to moment. She's even led agency wide sessions on self-care and exercise.

Volunteers who work for Martha love that she cares about their needs. During workshops and events she introduces volunteers to one another, helping them to learn about and get to know each other. Martha is also very attuned to those around her by listening and observing, which makes her a great program director for volunteers.

Martha's emotional and social intelligences are high, which makes it difficult for Lorraine, Martha's direct supervisor, to understand why Martha has such challenges working with people of cultural groups different than her own. Martha, as her jovial self, is always kind and thoughtful, but sometimes she will say culturally inappropriate things, not aware that she's said them.

One of the volunteers who is Southeast Asian has noted, "I like Martha but it seems like she just doesn't understand me. Like the time I had to cancel my tutoring shift. No one was watching my sister's baby so I had to watch her. I told Martha and she was real nice and understanding, but I feel that she didn't *really* understand that I have an obligation to my family before this volunteer job. I had to explain to her that this is what it's like in my culture, that family comes first. Then, she nodded and understood."

In this case, although Martha is empathic, she does not understand that the volunteer has very specific cultural needs. Her empathy is not viewed as authentic because Martha does not understand, nor does she pick up on, the cultural cues, thus leading the volunteer to feel the way she feels. Empathy is a good foundation for intercultural relationships, but awareness of cultural nuances is critical for making the connection.

The following describes other ways in which scholars and practitioners believe cultural intelligence is different from other approaches:

- Cultural intelligence is a growing field that is continuously being researched and tested in many societies. A search on the Internet for the word "cultural intelligence" yields over 2.7 million hits. When searching for academic papers and scholarship, the word yields almost 1.5 million hits. Other intercultural approaches do not yield as much universal appeal as cultural intelligence.

- Cultural intelligence demands that leaders gather more than knowledge of cultural facts. It is awareness of how culture works, of the values and beliefs that ground a person's thinking and motivation, and of exploring behavioral intelligence.

- Cultural intelligence emphasizes a circular path, not a linear one; this means that, over time, one will continue to learn and their cultural intelligence will expand. It is not a step-by-step process that culminates in an "ultimate outcome." Rather, through cultural intelligence, one learns more about him- or herself and his or her ability to interact with different cultures. There is always room for improvement and development in cultural intelligence.

- Cultural intelligence does not speak to specific cultures. Cultural intelligence is a broad approach that looks at developing a set of skills, as well as awareness and knowledge, that help you to adapt and interact with multiple cultures.

The Labyrinth of Cultural Intelligence

We have not even to risk the adventure alone. . . . the labyrinth is thoroughly known. We have only to follow the thread of the hero path. . . . and where we had thought to slay another, we shall slay ourselves. Where we had thought to travel outward, we will come to the center of our existence. And where we had thought to be alone, we will be with all the world.

—Joseph Campbell, *The Power of Myth*

Labyrinths often serve as metaphors for personal journeys into the self and back into the world. In a labyrinth, there is one path to the center, and that same path leads you out. You make the choice to enter the path and start a journey. You make the choice to continue the journey or to end it by retracing your steps to the place you entered.

You can think about your journey into cultural intelligence as entering a labyrinth. It is not a maze; rather, it is journey that brings you to a deeper awareness of yourself and your place in the world. In a labyrinth, you find yourself walking around short curves, long curves, around edges of the circle, getting closer to the center. As you do so, you may feel a variety of emotions and thought: hesitation, confidence, motivation, ease, caution, or reflection. In the labyrinth, we become the observer of these thoughts and emotions. As Carlson noted, "We can simply step back and watch the show. It's really just like watching a movie on the screen."[14]

The labyrinth has long served as a metaphor of change and growth. Walking the labyrinth is a time of exploration and discovery. Careful listening and the willingness to take risks, and to challenge yourself, lead you to a transformation. This transformation encompasses a new, expansive vision of possibilities in your world. It serves as a container for your experiences in life: fun and play, disappointment and sadness, grief and loss, joy and prosperity, success and failure. When you look at the labyrinth as a metaphor for your cultural intelligence journey, you will see that your path is sometimes shared with others, and, at times, it is yours alone.

As Joseph Campbell noted, everyone goes through a psychological transformation that brings them to a more fulfilling life.[15] Cultural intelligence is a process and a tool to help you evolve, to help you take the risks required when in unfamiliar cultural interactions. When applied, you will notice that you have gained a new consciousness of your place in the world.

Chapter Summary

- Cultural intelligence is the ability to adapt successfully to unfamiliar cultural settings.
- There are three elements to cultural intelligence: metacognition and cognition, motivation, and behavior.
- Cultural intelligence can be expressed as the ABCs of CI: acquire (knowledge), build (strategic thinking), contemplate (motivation), and do (behavior).
- Cultural intelligence is more comprehensive than emotional and social intelligences.
- People who have high emotional and social intelligences do not necessarily have high cultural intelligence.

- CI is more than knowledge-gathering; it does not speak to one specific culture.
- Your journey into cultural intelligence can be seen as entering a labyrinth. Labyrinths serve as metaphors for personal journeys that lead to transformation and change.
- Practicing and applying cultural intelligence principles enables you to learn more about yourself and your relationship to the world.

CHAPTER 4

Thinking About Thinking

Cultural strategic thinking is your ability to think and solve problems in specific ways when you are in unfamiliar cultural settings. To understand cultural strategic thinking, it is important for you to comprehend the two elements that make up this foundational piece of cultural intelligence: *cognition* and *metacognition*.

What Is Cognition?

Cognition is generally thought of as your ability to process information. As related to culture, you can think about it as the complete knowledge and experience you have gained about cultural situations and your interactions within those situations. Additionally, how you have thought about or processed this information is stored in your memory. Your ability to retrieve this stored information is defined as cognitive ability.

For example, I was conducting a workshop on cultural intelligence for educators, and one of the senior managers raised a question about proper etiquette in Southeast Asian cultures, particularly Lao and Hmong, that were present in her school district. She said, "I heard from one of my colleagues that it's considered rude if you touched or patted a child's head; that it's sacred. I tell my staff never to do this. Am I telling them the right cultural information?"

I replied that, *yes*, in some Southeast Asian cultures, touching or patting someone on the head is considered rude. "But, you have to realize that cultural information may not be true for every Southeast Asian child or parent you meet. Your awareness of this fact and your experiences related to this fact is a good thing to recall, but what if your new situation doesn't fit into your past experiences and what you know? What do you do?"

What I pointed out to her was that her awareness of this cultural fact was not enough. Earley and Peterson[1] stated that providing training in specific cognitive knowledge for multiple cultures is impractical. What is critical is equipping a manager with metacognitive skills so that, with time and experience, he or she can acquire new information concerning the cultural issues present in his or her team. With cultural intelligence, when the information you have does not fit a new situation, you have to be able to take in new information and reformulate it. Given this new information, you need to be flexible enough to reorganize how you think about the situation and the cultural fact(s) you have stored in your memory.

Throughout my educational and consulting sessions, I meet with people who are most concerned about "getting cultural facts and information correct." By this I mean they are interested in "what they can and can't do," or "making sure they act within the boundaries of proper behaviors." Some even want a "10 commandments of cultural etiquette." As a result, most people end up with cultural facts and information that help them understand the culture, but not the ability to work with, and adapt to, the culture.

The reality is, when you are working on a multinational team or supervising and leading a multinational staff, you need to have a higher level of thinking (cognition). This is where cultural strategic thinking really matters and where metacognition becomes important.

What Is Metacognition?

Metacognition refers to "thinking about thinking" and was introduced as a concept by John Flavell, who is typically seen as a founding scholar of the field. Flavell said that metacognition is the knowledge you have of your own cognitive processes (your thinking).[2] It is your ability to control your thinking processes through various strategies, such as organizing, monitoring, and adapting. Additionally, it is your ability to reflect upon the tasks or processes you undertake and to select and utilize the appropriate strategies necessary in your intercultural interactions.

Metacognition is considered a critical component of successful learning. It involves self-regulation and self-reflection of strengths, weaknesses, and the types of strategies you create. It is a necessary foundation in culturally intelligent leadership because it underlines how you think through a problem or situation and the strategies you create to address the situation or problem.

Many people become accustomed to having trainers and consultants provide them with knowledge about cultures to the point where they are dependent on the coach, mentor, trainer, or consultant. However, they need to learn to be experts in cultural situations themselves through metacognitive strategies such as adapting, monitoring, self-regulation, and self-reflection. Culturally intelligent leaders can use metacognition to help themselves and to train themselves to think through their thinking.

Metacognition is broken down into three components: metacognitive knowledge, metacognitive experience, and metacognitive strategies. Each of these is discussed in the following sections.

Metacognitive Knowledge

Metacognitive knowledge involves (a) *learning processes* and your beliefs about how you learn and how you think others learn, (b) the *task of learning* and how you process information, and (c) the *strategies* you develop and when you will use them. Let's say you have to learn a new language in 6 months. Here is how you would think about it, using metacognitive knowledge:

- *Learning Process*: I am good at learning new languages and I think I can do this in the time period I have been given.
- *Task of Learning*: To complete this task, I will need to think about the following:
  - How soon can I get information to start learning the language?
  - How long will it take me to learn the language?
  - What information is available to me to learn this new language?
  - Is this language similar to a language I *have* learned before?
  - Will I be able to learn the language in time?
  - How hard will it be for me to learn this language?
  - What do I need to do to learn the language?
- *The Strategies*: I think learning this new language is going to take me 12 months, but I only have 6 months to prepare. I

better find other ways to me meet this goal. I think I will find out if there is an accelerated language class that I can take. Maybe I should consider hiring a private tutor, or maybe I will just focus on learning the basics of the language.

Metacognitive Experience

Arnold Bennett, a British writer, said that one cannot have knowledge without having emotions.[3] In metacognition, there are feelings and emotions present that are related to the goals and tasks of learning. These components of metacognition speak to metacognitive experience, which is your internal response to learning. Your feelings and emotions serve as a feedback system to help you understand your progress and expectations, and your comprehension and connection of new information to the old, among other things.

When you learn a new language, for example, you may recall memories, information, and earlier experiences in your life to help you solve the task of learning a new language. In doing this, your internal responses (metacognitive experience) could be frustration, disappointment, happiness, or satisfaction. Each of these internal responses can affect the task of learning a new language and determine your willingness to continue. Critical to metacognition is the ability to deliberately foster a positive attitude and positive feelings toward your learning.

Metacognitive Strategies

Metacognitive strategies are what you design to monitor your progress related to your learning and the tasks at hand. It is a mechanism for controlling your thinking activities and to ensure you are meeting your goals. Metacognitive strategies for learning a new language can include the following:

- monitoring whether you understand the language lessons;
- recognizing when you fail to comprehend information communicated to you in the new language;
- identifying strategies that help you to improve your comprehension;

- adjusting your pace for learning the information (for example, studying for 2 hours, rather than 1 hour, every day);
- maintaining the attitude necessary to ensure you complete the lessons in a timely manner;
- creating a check-in system at the end of each week to make certain you understand what you have learned.

As one business manager of a Fortune 300 company told me,

> Understanding cultural strategic thinking is like this: When I work with people of different cultures, this is a framework and approach to help me understand how I think when I work with them. It helps me to recognize the cultural experiences I've had, and to identify preconceived notions I might have about their culture, whether it's race/ethnicity, social culture, age group—you name it. Cultural strategic thinking forces me to create experiences and new learning that helps me to accomplish my objectives as a global manager.[4]

Individuals like this leader are good at applying strategies that focus their attention on the goal at hand. They search for, and derive meaning from, cultural interactions and situations, and they adapt themselves to the situation when things do not pan out as they expected. Culturally intelligent leaders also monitor and direct their own learning processes. They have established a high motivation for learning the metacognitive process, either because they know it is a benefit or because others tell them it is beneficial to them.

Knowledge of factual information and basic skills provides a foundation for developing metacognition. Metacognition enables leaders to master information and solve problems more easily. When a leader has mastered the basic skills needed for intercultural interactions, they can actively engage in the interaction because they do not have to pay attention to the other dynamics and demands of the situation. Culturally intelligent leaders are able to practice metacognition, and they are not afraid to use it in their everyday life.

For those who lack basic intercultural skills, it is more difficult for them to engage in the interaction. They are more occupied with finding the "right information," the "right skills," and the "right facts" needed to solve the problem. In such situations, these types of leaders spend little time developing their metacognitive skills, and the result is likely an inefficient solution to a problem. Developing a laundry list or checklist of do's and don'ts will not assist leaders in improving their cultural intelligence.

Techniques for Developing Strategic Thinking

How can you improve your strategic thinking? Basic strategies for improving thinking include (a) connecting new information with what you already know, (b) selecting your thinking strategies carefully and intentionally, and (c) planning, monitoring, and evaluating your thinking strategies and processes.

Connecting New Information

Strategic thinking is "thinking about thinking." It *is* being conscious of your thinking processes, such as how you have gathered and organized the information and experience in your memory (old information), and then how you reorganize it (new information) to fit a new situation. You have to connect the new information to what you already know in order to help make sense of what actions to take. You can do this by identifying what you know and what you do not know about a cultural situation. Here is an exercise to help you identify old and new information. Take a sheet a paper and draw a line down the middle of the sheet to create two columns. At the top of the left column, write, "What I know," and at the top of the right column, write, "What I want to learn." As you research, explore, and interact with a cultural situation, people, or information, you will learn to clarify, revise, verify, or expand your understanding of the situation.

Let us look at the example of Betty, who is a product manager for a local distributor of processed foods and snacks. With a growing Hispanic population that has an increasingly large purchasing power in the United States, her company wants to expand into the market and seize this opportunity and potential for growth. This is not a new market for the business, but it requires that her team think strategically about what they know and do not know about this consumer base.

Table 4.1. Identification of Knowledge Gaps

What I Know	What I Want to Learn
• Between the years 1991–2013, the projected growth of Hispanic purchasing power is 560%. • Hispanics are the largest minority group in the United States. • By 2020, the U.S. Hispanic population will triple. • Family is central to Hispanic communities • A large percentage of Hispanic families are from low-income families.	• Differences in lifestyles among Hispanic groups. • Reasons for immigration or coming to the United States. • Cultural etiquette in doing business with Hispanics. • History of Hispanic culture in the United States.

Next, Betty and her team will need identify the strategies that will help them to be more intentional with their work.

Selecting Intentional Thinking Strategies

Based on this exercise, Betty has identified strategies that will connect new information to the old in the ways shown in Figure 4.1.

By connecting old information with the new, Betty is making conscious choices and decisions about what she knows and what she does not know. This sets her up with strategies that are most appropriate for her. Strategic thinking is most useful when you find strategies that work appropriately for your level of knowledge, building upon what you know.

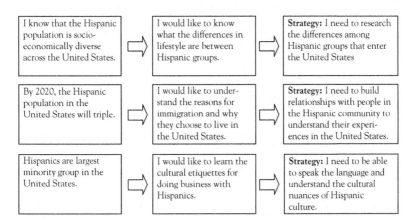

Figure 4.1. Creating intentional strategies.

As indicated earlier in the chapter, if this new knowledge is basic information and Betty does not have this, she can be easily distracted, which may create interruptions in her learning and practice of strategic thinking.

Planning, Monitoring, and Evaluating

As Betty collects information related to her actions, she will add or revise her strategies, as needed, because her knowledge base has grown and what was "new information" at one time is now old information. Betty will put in place strategies that help her to monitor her progress toward her goal as well as to evaluate how she thinks about each strategy. Because the information is new to her, and if the information is basic knowledge that she needs, she will need to pay attention to her mind's ability to be easily distracted. When she is aware of this, she can retrain her brain to identify the distraction and then refocus on her goals. There are a variety of strategies she can use to plan, monitor, and evaluate her progress.

One strategy Betty has employed is to create the time and space with her team to discuss her cultural experiences. This allows her to process, out loud, the knowledge she has obtained and forces her to think about her thinking, that is, her metacognition. Because she puts this strategy in place, she can understand what her mind is processing during her learning, and she is then able to identify and focus on her strengths and improve upon her weaknesses. When she does this with a group, her peers help her to learn about her thinking while she helps them to learn about their learning processes.

Cultural Strategic Thinking Techniques

The basics of developing and practicing cultural strategic thinking are to (a) connect new information to the old, (b) select the appropriate strategies, and then (c) plan, monitor, and evaluate the strategies you have put in place. This section of the chapter provides ideas that will help you to increase your cultural strategic thinking.

Peer Learning

A strategy that is often employed in the practice of cultural strategic thinking is to create peer-learning opportunities to explore cultural interactions and resolve cultural problems. Doing this provides you with a language for how you process cultural interactions and problems, and your peers can help you to create that language and help solve the problems. As a leader, this is a great way of providing a model for those who have difficulty with cultural strategic thinking. It does so by sharing with them a language and a process, and by helping to point out the cultural strategic thinking pieces of the process, which can be done by asking and clarifying the situation for them. Think about it as playing cultural detective: You ask your peers questions, and they clarify the information for you, and when they ask you questions, you clarify your thinking process for them.

Writing Your Experiences

A useful tool I have used in my workshops and classes is writing down experiences and thoughts related to a cultural situation. I encourage you to write down your emotions and feelings, the ambiguities and inconsistencies, and the challenges and successes of working interculturally. Your writing serves as a reflection of your thinking processes and how you have dealt with, or how you could not deal with, the process. It also serves as a memory of your experiences, which you can later refer back to and learn from.

Gaining Cultural Knowledge

In gaining cultural knowledge, it is very helpful to get into the habit of checking your facts and knowledge about a culture. You can do this by using multiple sources and venues. If you come across a situation in which a cultural fact seems to contradict what you know, take the time to learn about the difference and the nuances related to that cultural fact. Using that cultural situation as a "Kodak moment," take the opportunity to reread the picture to see if you really understood how that cultural fact was used. In your review of the situation, you may need to research unfamiliar terms or gestures used, or you may need to break down the picture and rebuild it, step by step, to understand if you really understood the whole picture.

Thinking, Being, and Staying Positive

Essential in cultural strategic thinking is your ability to conjure up and be positive about your learning experiences. Someone who holds a negative perspective about, or who had a negative experience, working with different cultural groups will continute to have difficulty working with the groups. Negative attitudes and impressions will hinder your work. You have to think positively about a situation, and you need to be and stay positive, maintaining a positive energy and attitude throughout. I have certainly come across leaders who have attended my sessions because "leadership told them they had to," and it affects their learning environment in a negative way and often interrupts the learning of their peers. Your ability to be a culturally intelligent leader depends on your willingness to maintain a positive attitude.

Finding a Coach or Mentor

Along the lines of processing your cultural situations out loud, it would be helpful to find a coach or mentor that can help you analyze your thinking. In cultural strategic thinking, it is important to talk about what you will do or what you have to do. Some people will talk to themselves; others find it helpful to have someone to talk to. As in peer learning, talking to someone else gives you the opportunity to break down your thinking processes.

Being an Observer

One of the best things to do in developing cultural strategic thinking is to learn to be an observer. Through observation and active listening, you pick up what you normally do not see. Observation is acquired through day-to-day activities in your life by making a conscious decision to be open and alert. Pay attention to the verbal and nonverbal cues of various situations; look around your environment and note the various symbols and artifacts. Culturally intelligent leaders must have excellent observation skills, never failing to hear and see the tangible and intangible. You can do this by reminding yourself or by setting goals centered around the following actions:

- Listen with an open mind
- Be open to new ideas
- Suspend judgments of people and their beliefs
- Ask people questions
- Silently ask yourself questions
- Be open to experiences that are unfamiliar

Active Listening

Active listening is your ability to understand, interpret, reflect on, and respond to what you have heard. It is a critical skill in cultural intelligence because the behavior acknowledges that you have really heard what another person has said. Active listening focuses your mind on the speaker, and, if done repeatedly and successfully, you are able to build trust and a relationship with others. It can facilitate an effective cultural interaction with less conflict, confusion, and frustration. Practicing to be an active listener is making a conscious choice about your responses to others. Because cultural intelligence is intentional, you are also better able to regulate your emotions and feelings.

Changing Your Questions

Marilee Adams[5] proposes that when you change your questions in any given situation, this allows you to change your thinking. There are two types of questions: questions that involve judgments and questions that involve learning. We ask both types of questions, and we choose which ones to ask in any given situation. Asking questions in a different way provides us with another perspective.

Table 4.2. Judger Versus Learner Questions

Judger	Learner
• What's wrong?	• What works?
• Who's to blame?	• What am I responsible for?
• How can I prove I'm right?	• What are the facts?
• How can I protect my turf?	• What's the big picture?
• How can I be in control?	• What are my choices?
• How could I lose?	• What's useful about this?
• How could I get hurt?	• What can I learn?
• Why is that person so clueless and frustrating?	• What is the other person feeling, needing, and wanting?
• Why bother?	• What's possible?

Note. Adapted from Marilee G. Adams, 2004, *Change your questions, change your life: 7 powerful tools for life and work*, San Francisco, CA: Berrett-Koehler, p. 49.

Cultural strategic thinking may seem overwhelming at first, but as with any new learning, you need to break your plan into smaller steps that will help you to accomplish your goals. When you get into the habit of cultural strategic thinking, you will begin thinking on an unconscious level and not even recognize that you are using strategic thinking. You will notice it when others marvel or comment at your ability to effectively manage cultural interactions.

Earley and Peterson[6] wrote that learning about a new culture requires putting all the pieces of a pattern together when you do not know the totality of what that whole picture should look like. Cultural strategic thinking is essential because it is this higher strategic thinking that enables you to process the new information and reinterpret it in a new situation. Cultural strategic thinking helps you to discard what you think you know and to apply new information concerning what the situation could be. By training your mind to think at a higher level, you create new maps of cultural situations, which help you to function more effectively.

Chapter Summary

- Leaders must be aware of how they process information related to culture and their ability to think about this thinking, which is called metacognition.
- Metacognition is an essential core of successful learning, and leaders who lack the basic knowledge about working with cultures will have more challenges in their ability to be culturally intelligent.
- Culturally intelligent leaders create strategies that help them focus on the goal of their cultural interactions. They use feedback from the situation and adapt it to create a new picture, while creating new learning patterns for themselves.
- Strategies that can help leaders build their strategic thinking include peer learning, coaching and mentoring, reflecting on their thinking processes in a journal or book, and being an observer and active listener.
- Strategic thinking techniques address the basic development skills necessary in metacognition: connection of new information to old, intentionally selecting the appropriate strategies necessary for that situation, and planning, monitoring, and evaluating the strategies and one's progress.

CHAPTER 5

I Think I Can and I Will

Why is it that some people are more willing and eager to work through intercultural challenges, while others seem unmotivated, disinterested, or unengaged? Why do some people demonstrate high levels of confidence, while others are anxious, feel insecure, or shy away from the challenges? The ability to meet your goals is your self-efficacy; how you manage your confidence and your emotions is emotional intelligence; and your willingness to reflect and consider your surroundings is called mindfulness. In this chapter of the book, these three concepts will be discussed in relationship to cultural intelligence.

What Is Self-Efficacy?

Self-efficacy, as defined by Albert Bandura,[1] represents your perception of your abilities to meet a goal you have set for yourself. It is similar to self-confidence. Self-efficacy is a foundational component in cultural intelligence. For the past 25 years, scholars have researched this topic and the strategies that leaders can use to encourage higher levels of efficacy in their employees.

People with lower self-efficacy will have challenges throughout intercultural processes because they do not believe that they will be able to solve the problem. They do not feel they have the skills needed to work through the issues. Conversely, leaders who have higher levels of self-efficacy believe they can overcome obstacles, whether difficult or not. They have an easier time engaging in problem solving and finding strategic approaches for solving the issues before them.

Table 5.1. Self-Efficacy Perspectives About Unfamiliar Cultural Settings

High Self-Efficacy Perspective About Unfamiliar Cultural Settings	Low Self-Efficacy Perspective About Unfamiliar Cultural Settings
• The task is to master unfamiliar settings • Sets higher commitment to goals and process • Internal motivation to work diligently • "If I fail, I'll try again" • Focus on success and removing obstacles • Visualize positive experiences and outcomes	• The task is "too big for me" to handle • No commitment to goals and process • Motivation is decreased; little to no effort • "It's too stressful, complicated, and frustrating." • Focus on obstacles and challenges • Visualize negative experiences and outcomes

The Role of Self-Efficacy in Cultural Intelligence

As a leader working with different and unfamiliar cultures, your self-efficacy determines how you think, feel, and behave in cultural situations. It is your beliefs about what you can and cannot do. It is your confidence level in intercultural situations and the results that it has on your ability to adapt to another culture. It is your belief that you have the ability to work through cultural issues that can contribute to your perseverance in daunting, challenging situations.

If you have a high level of self-efficacy, you are not afraid to take on cultural challenges. Instead, you perceive the tasks involved as if they are something to be mastered. Your belief stirs up an internal motivation for you to be successful and to fully engage in the problem. You are more likely to set challenging goals and diligently work through activities. You are also more apt to maintain a commitment to the process and the goals. When the going gets tough, you keep on going because of your perseverance and resiliency. Take, for example, the case of Jerry and Mingxia:

> Jerry works in a large university and has managed the day-to-day operations of the study abroad center for three years. Because of the focus on studying abroad, many of the students who work in the center are from outside the United States. Most recently, Jerry hired a student from China for a work study position coordinating front desk activities. Jerry has enjoyed working with Mingxia

thus far, but he has noticed that when he needs tasks to be accomplished, she doesn't give him a definite "yes" or "no" and sometimes provides an ambiguous response to his questions. He's quickly realizing that when she says "yes," it means she understood him but it doesn't mean she agrees. At first he is frustrated, but that frustration gives way to interest and fascination about cultural differences. He's had to sit down with her several times to discuss the tasks, but he approaches the conversation as a learning opportunity for him and her. He realizes that managing this cultural interaction is necessary for the work of the department. He has found that even though it takes more effort to build cultural understanding, he has seen it pay off. The other day, Mingxia brought in her friends who were interested in working with the center because they heard it was a great working environment and that he was a great boss.

Jerry's perception of cultural challenges was to change them into opportunities; he adapted to the situation at hand. This is a vastly different response than what would be observed in a person with a lower self-efficacy. These individuals tend to doubt their abilities in unfamiliar cultural settings. They tend to avoid challenging situations and often visualize potential failures and setbacks. Individuals with low self-efficacy attribute their failures to not having the right competencies or information for the situation, whereas those who have high self-efficacy attribute failures to not putting in the right amount of effort required.

Using the cultural intelligence (CI) model in Figure 3.1, Jerry can think about this situation in this way:

- Acquire: Jerry needs to acquire cultural knowledge to help him understand the situation better. He already knows from his interactions with Mingxia that language, particularly responding with "yes" and "no," may not be productive in this case. He also knows that Mingxia is from China and has connected his department with future employees. Jerry also could learn more about students from China and in particular, how they like to work with someone who is older than them.
- Build: In this situation, Jerry can use what he knows and what he would like know to create new ways to interact with

Mingxia. He may have to try the strategies and test them out. A culturally intelligent leader would think about how he could plan, monitor, and evaluate his strategies. During the process, he learns what works for Mingxia and what does not. For example, Jerry may want to try asking Mingxia questions that are not closed ended or require "yes/no" responses.

- Contemplate: Along with his strategies, he may remind himself to pay attention to Mingxia's verbal and nonverbal cues. He could try either or both of these strategies, paying attention to his surroundings—both the visible and invisible pieces of culture; as he receives a response, he will adapt as needed. During the contemplation stage, Jerry can choose to suspend his judgments. When he notices he has judgments or a negative emotion is present, he can take a step back to listen and recognize what cultural scripts are occurring.

- Do: As he interacts with Mingxia on a daily basis, he can learn to apply the fourth principle of CI. He can do this by asking himself how he might appear to Mingxia. Is he too authoritative? Too accommodating? Did he use words that were unclear? Was he too direct? These questions can help Jerry to use CI principles on a daily basis, and as a result, he learns more about himself and builds his self-efficacy.

Jerry's self-efficacy helps him to be a better culturally intelligent leader. When doubt is present in individuals it detracts from one's efforts. People with lower self-efficacy give up more easily and lower their expectations and goals. They see situations as not only uncomfortable but also, in some cases, threatening. Avoiding uncomfortable and threatening situations is a top priority for these individuals because it produces more anxiety, stress, disorientation, and frustration. Unfamiliar cultural situations become stressful and can be depressing. The following is an example of an American educator assigned to work with an Iraqi family:

Melissa is meeting Ashraf's parents to discuss his progress in class. This is the first time she is meeting his parents, who have emigrated from the Middle East recently. When they arrive late to the meeting, she greets the father by offering to shake his hand, as common in American society. He looks puzzled and shakes her hand. Then, Melissa turns to the mother and proceeds to shake her hand. Ashraf's mother looks at Melissa, very confused, and then looks at her husband. A few seconds pass, but eventually she reaches out to shake Melissa's hand.

During the conversation with Ashraf's parents, Melissa asks both parents questions about Ashraf's home life. She wants to get a sense of how Ashraf is using the information he has learned in class in his home environment. Throughout the meeting, Melissa senses that the father is becoming more impatient and suspicious, and she is uncertain as to why. She notices that the father dominates the conversation and responds to the questions she poses to the mother. He also seems evasive when responding to her.

Melissa is beginning to feel very frustrated with the father. She finds herself repeating a lot of what she's said and explaining to the parents the reason for the meeting. Halfway through the meeting she knows she isn't going to accomplish what she initially set out to do. She's dreading a second meeting with the family, and she's becoming more and more impatient with the father. Why would he treat his wife like that? Doesn't he realize that she can answer for herself? For the rest of the meeting, Melissa loses her focus and finds herself thinking about other things. The meeting ends earlier than scheduled, but she's more than happy that the meeting is over.

After the meeting, Melissa shares the experience with her colleagues. She says, "The dad was always interrupting and the mom was really quiet. I'm pretty sure she's scared to disagree with him. Now, I have to meet them again because I didn't even get what I needed from them. This second meeting better not be a waste of my time. It's not like we have the luxury in this job to meet parents whenever they want."

Melissa's thoughts and actions revealed her stress and her level of discomfort with the situation. Because this is the first time Melissa has met with a Middle Eastern family, she does not know the proper cultural etiquette. She may not be aware of the cultural information she needs ahead of time to work with the family, which may explain why she does not pick up on the mother's hesitation when shaking hands. Additionally,

Melissa uses judgments based on her cultural values system to explain the uncertainty she feels. For example, she finds the father to be suspicious and evasive. How does she know that what she sees is a representation of suspicious and evasive behavior? She only knows what she sees based on her cultural experiences—her cultural lens.

Notice that in the latter half of the meeting, Melissa lowers her expectations and focuses her attention elsewhere. This is evident of her thinking, which implies that her cultural experiences are the only ways to interpret the world. Rather than taking responsibility for how the meeting was run, she puts the blame and responsibility on the family. To her, the father's constant interruptions and the mother's silence represented disregard for her objectives; thus, her comment, "It's not like we have a luxury in this job to meet parents whenever they want."

What can be done to help Melissa improve her self-efficacy? Using the principles of CI, Melissa can think about future cultural interactions in this way:

- Acquire: Melissa can identify what she knows and does not know about Middle Eastern culture and in particular, Iraqi culture and customs. By identifying these areas, she creates a chart of her knowledge. Culturally intelligent leaders need to know what gaps exist for them when they interact with different cultures. In this case, Melissa will need to start at the basics, not just learning about Iraqi culture; she needs to learn about her own culture in order to understand how Iraqi families may be different from her own.

- Build: Melissa can build her knowledge of the culture by gathering information from different sources such as books, documentaries, attending local events, or speaking with someone who knows about the culture. These are strategies she builds for herself to understand more about Iraqi culture. Some of these may be challenging to her because she may have never tried the strategies or activities before. But, as she conducts the activities, she can pay attention to how she feels and what she is thinking. By doing this, she will understand where her level of comfort is and where she needs to be challenged.

- Contemplate: When applying this component of CI, Melissa may create a goal for herself to listen more to families' nonverbal cues. Paying attention to this enables her to suspend her assumptions. She may even reflect on what assumptions come up for her before, during, and after meeting with families. In contemplation, Melissa may reflect on her own motivation to helping families. How committed is she to helping all families, no matter their ethnic background? How motivated is she to keep trying even when she feels uncomfortable? These are some questions that she can ask herself and then find solutions to, moving her forward in a positive manner.

- Do: Melissa's work in this particular CI element is to observe her own behaviors with families from different cultural backgrounds. As she practices her strategies, she can monitor and evaluate whether the behavior was appropriate or not by observing the responses from others. By checking her level of adaptability in the meetings, she will learn to mimic and mirror the appropriate cultural gestures and cues.

Emotional Intelligence and Self-Efficacy

Have you ever been to a busy mall, event, or festival during the busiest time of the season, and you could not find a parking spot? Driving all around, let us say that you finally located a spot, only to find that you cannot park there because there is a car that double-parked in that space. What is your reaction? What if this situation consistently happens to you and the parking lot is in a different city or state, a different region of the country, or another country all together? What is your reaction then? What assumptions would you make about the people who drive the car? What assumptions might you have about the people who live in that city, state, region, or country?

In cultural intelligence, a development of high self-efficacy is necessary in unfamiliar cultural environments. You do not have a choice but to develop a higher self-efficacy. This area of the human potential is spoken about in the study of emotional intelligence. Daniel Goleman[2] was the first to popularize the concept of emotional intelligence (EI). Building on the work of John Mayer and Peter Salovey, Goleman distilled EI into a relatively concise set of five skills, addressed in the following questions:

- How well do you *know* your emotions?
- How well do you *manage* your emotions?

- How do you *adapt or change* based on your emotions?
- How well do you *recognize* the emotions in others?
- How well do you *handle* relationships?

Self-management of emotions plays a critical role in leadership. As Goleman notes, managing emotions is a full-time job[3]. For leaders, self-management encompasses a multitude of competencies that include emotional self-control, that is, the ability to stay calm and clear-headed during periods of high stress or during a crisis. It is important for leaders to develop ways of dealing with their disruptive impulses and emotions, especially in intercultural situations.

Self-efficacy requires adaptability and initiative. Adaptability is your ability to juggle multiple demands, adapt to new challenges, and adjust to new changes. Adaptability allows you to effectively deal with the ambiguities of cultures. Your initiative is your competency to seize the challenges and turn them into opportunities. You create and act rather than wait.

Learning to develop an optimistic perspective will help you to improve your self-efficacy, thus improving your ability to be resilient to challenges. You begin to see the best in people and expect that changes will be positive. For example, Viktor Frankl, a man who survived the horrific experiences of the concentration camps in Nazi Germany, noted that even though he had suffered, he chose to see his experiences in the camps as one that held meaning for him. He said that choosing your own attitude in any situation is one of the most powerful freedoms provided to mankind.[4]

Frankl shows that choosing one's attitude can shift one's perspective, thus creating new possibilities. His thinking on this subject matter has been instrumental in opening up new possibilities of thinking about the capacity of human beings to survive and find meaning in life. His book *Man's Search for Meaning* provides a platform for existential therapy and logotherapy.

Mindfulness and Self-Efficacy

What is *mindfulness*? According to Boyatzis and McKee, mindfulness "is the capacity to be fully aware of all that one experiences *inside the self*—body, mind, heart, spirit—and to pay full attention to what is happening *around us*—people, the natural world, our surroundings, and events."[5] Ajahn Sumedho,[6] in *Teachings of a Buddhist Monk*, wrote that mindfulness is about a full awareness of what is going on inside; it's not necessarily about concentrating on a particular object or thing, because our concentration does not last long. Rather, being *mindful* means allowing for the experience of the moment to arise, whether that experience is confusion, hurt, laughter, or excitement.

Many people equate the concept of mindfulness to Eastern philosophers who look at mindfulness as a process of self-awareness that directs the self to take part in being in the "present moment." This reflective process is nonjudgmental, meaning that mindfulness is accepting whatever is happening. Mindfulness is not *thinking* in terms of categorizing experiences or labeling them; rather, it allows the experiences to just be. It does not associate with the ego—"I," "me," and "mine." Instead, it looks at only the experience(s) in the present moment from an objective stance or that of an observer. In this way, mindfulness provides experiences so profound that it can, and has, changed perspectives and relationships.

Mindfulness has been shown to be effective in innovation and creativity. The phrase "think outside of the box" eludes to mindfulness. To "think outside of the box" means that you cannot categorize, label, or see the issue or object in the same perspective as you did before. You must choose a different way to look at what is in front of you. This would mean that you need to challenge yourself to do things outside of your comfort zone, and, oftentimes, you are doing something you would not even think about doing. In this way, mindfulness is a process, not an outcome.

Culturally intelligent leaders who use mindfulness are generally more open to possibilities and different perspectives. They allow themselves to receive new information even if they believe that what is in front of them is indeed fact or true to them. A state of mindfulness helps to create possibilities and different avenues for growth. Take, for example, the following situation:

Two politicians from opposing parties are in disagreement about actions to take regarding a potential new immigration policy. Both politicians recognize that there is an immigration issue in the country and that it has a significant impact on the economy. Both believe that controlling immigration into the country is the key to maintaining national security and ensures the health and well-being of the country's citizens. One of the politicians believes that a way to control immigration is to round up all illegal immigrants and deport them. The other politician believes that only specific illegal immigrants should return to their country. Enter a third politician who has been listening to the argument. This politician sees both sides of the arguments and recognizes the truth in each statement. As a result of mindful listening, receiving, and reflection, this politician offers a third alternative that may contain components of the two opposing arguments or it could be a completely different way of thinking about immigration.

Mindfulness techniques help you to come to an awareness of your self-efficacy. Through mindfulness, you learn to see your perspective of a situation, whether objects, people, places, or ideas are involved. The connection between mindfulness and self-efficacy is such that when you use mindfulness, it helps you to focus on your performance and goals.

This next exercise is to help you use mindfulness to accomplish a goal. On a piece of paper, write down one goal you have (i.e., "My goal is to . . ."). This may be related to work, your family, your finances, starting a new business, purchasing a new car—anything you would like to obtain. Below your stated goal, write down five things you plan on doing to achieve this goal. Next, have two people (e.g., friends, neighbors, strangers) each write down five things you can do to achieve this goal. Then, review what you have written down to achieve your goal as well as what others have said for you to do to reach your goal. Now, respond to the following questions:

- How would you react if none of the plans you made turned out the way they were supposed to?
- What if, in the middle of working toward your goal, the goal changed?
- If you reached your goal exactly as you planned it, what would you have learned about yourself?
- What type of life do you think you would lead if everything went according to your plans?

Asking these questions not only helps you to be more mindful, it helps you to be more focused on your goals.

Mindlessness and Self-Efficacy

We make every effort to keep things as they are, because human beings, alone, lament transience. Yet no matter how we grieve or protest, there is no way to impede the flow of anything. If we but see things as they are and flow with them, we may find enjoyment in transience. Because human life is transient, all manner of figures are woven into its fabric.

—Shundo Aoyama, *Zen Seeds*

Ellen Langer[7] wrote that we are all capable of *mindfulness*, as well as its counterpart, *mindlessness*. We subconsciously take part in mindlessness, out of habit or repetition, or out of our own self-placed limitations; however, if we focused on mindfulness, we would, in fact, be able to change our perspective of ourselves, our situations, our environment, or our world. Mindlessness can lock us into a specific way of being, thinking, and acting. We are not even aware that we are mindless unless we are in a situation where our mindlessness is challenged or we are conscious of being mindful.

Similar to this concept is the famous analogy of the cave by the Greek philosopher Plato. The analogy describes prisoners chained up in a cave, facing its wall; they have been there all their lives. They can only see shadows of animals, people, or other objects that pass by the entrance of the cave. Because they have never seen the outside of the cave, they do not know what is real except what they see in front of them. In other words, they accept the shadows as reality. However, one person breaks free from the chains and is able to see that the realities of the shadows—the objects, people, or animals behind the shadows—are real. He returns to tell the others about this new reality but is scorned and ridiculed. No one believes that there is another reality besides what they see in front of them.

Mindlessness occurs because we are accustomed to categorizing things in a way that does not allow for alternative possibilities. We automatically think in terms of limitations; therefore, we limit ourselves in our thinking and behavior. For example, a short person who, for all of his life, feels that his height limits and hinders him can never escape the category he has created for himself—that is that he is short. Even if others do not see the same reality as he does, his own reality is so strong that it affects his behavior and, ultimately, his sense of self-worth. It is the same with a woman who has been repeatedly told that she is stupid and worthless.

She begins to see that this is the only way to live and starts to act out behaviors that mirror what she has been told.

Mindlessness can then lead to learned helplessness, a term that describes a state of futility after having experienced multiple failures. For example, if a mother constantly makes her daughter's bed in the morning, and the mother tells her daughter that the only person who can make the bed the correct way is a mother figure, then the daughter will learn that she cannot make her own bed or even that she is incapable of making a bed. What if the mother decides that she no longer wants to make her daughter's bed? The daughter could make her own bed, but she may also reveal that she does not know how to make a bed and that the only person who could make a bed is a mother figure.

Learned helplessness can also appear in cultural interactions. A number of times, I have met people who believe that "working with other cultures is too difficult," and, as a result, their behaviors, their words, and their attitudes speak to this. This mentality perpetuates their behaviors and their inability to escape this learned helplessness. They give up quickly, they make excuses, or they justify their beliefs. By repeating movements, actions, behaviors, words, or thoughts, we enter a state of mindlessness. The tasks we have repeated become an unconscious part of us like driving, brushing our teeth, or eating.

The following exercises will assist you in thinking about how repetitive exercises can contribute to mindlessness and what the consequences of repetitive actions are:

- Recite the alphabet; then, recite the alphabet backwards.
- Sing the words to *Twinkle, Twinkle, Little Star*. Next, sing every other word to the song.
- On a piece of paper, write down what you noticed when you recited the alphabet backwards and when you skipped every other word of *Twinkle, Twinkle, Little Star*.
- Write a short note to a friend using your dominant hand. Now, using the nondominant hand, write the same short note to a friend. Write down what you noticed when you switched to your nondominant hand.

Developing Your Self-Efficacy

This section outlines practical approaches you can use in your daily life to help increase your self-efficacy, your emotional intelligence, and your capacity to be mindful.

Identify Moments of Success

You should identify experiences when you have successfully worked with cultures other than your own. You can also cultivate environments where you can be successful. Creating environments to practice and learn from your mistakes is essential for culturally intelligent leaders. When you build a space for others to learn, you encourage their sense of self-efficacy. You help to minimize their doubts about working with others, thus reducing their stress. However, focusing on creating easy successes can foster an environment where the individual comes to expect easy results. Find opportunities that both challenge and create success.

Teach and Promote Resilience

You can create a strong sense of efficacy by purposefully teaching resiliency. As a leader, it is about teaching others how they can bounce back from failures. Everyone needs to learn that they have what it takes to be successful in making it through difficulties. You can teach resiliency by promoting and pointing out positive behaviors and attitudes. It is also about helping those you lead to identify when they are using negative self-talk. The following case illustrates a leader teaching and promoting resilience with her employee.

> Theresa, a senior sales manager, knows that a new hire, Jane, is new to working with a Hispanic population. What Jane knows about the population is based on media sources, research and papers she's read, and what she's picked up over time from her social network. Jane has a lot of work ahead of her if she wants to understand and work well with this consumer base.
>
> Theresa provides constructive feedback to Jane in a variety of ways that encourages her to keep her motivation and interest

high. She compliments Jane on things she does well and often says, "You're making great progress." Although there are times when Jane just doesn't seem to "get it" as fast as she should, Theresa believes that eventually, with training and the proper resources, Jane will succeed. Recently, Jane came back to the office with a big smile on her face. She was able to negotiate and secure a contract with a business in the Hispanic community. Theresa immediately congratulates her. "That's fantastic. Way to go! Tell me all about it."

As Jane recalls the experience, Theresa follows up with questions and prompts to convey her support and enthusiasm. When Jane recalls a minor setback in her conversation with the business, Theresa says, "Wait now. Don't underestimate what you were able to do. That's a minor issue and I know that if you secured the contract you must have adequately addressed that with the client."

Jane hesitates, and then nods her head. "You're right. I did. He seemed real relaxed after I explained it to him."

Theresa notices the hesitation. To ensure that Jane realizes her good effort paid off, Theresa says, "Good work! Now that you've had this experience, what lessons learned can you take to your next sales opportunity?"

Theresa provides teaching moments of resiliency to Jane. As a culturally intelligent leader should, she is helping Jane learn the value of not giving up in the face of difficulty. She also points out the negative self-talk (verbal and nonverbal) that Jane slips into the conversation. Theresa ends the conversation on a positive note, continuing to show interest and support of Jane's progress.

As Theresa is teaching Jane, she also learns about her own resiliency. Working with Jane is a new cultural experience for her: She is working with someone who is unfamiliar with certain aspects of her job and the consumers. As a person with many responsibilities, and one holding a position of leadership and authority in the organization, Theresa does not have a lot of time to manage Jane. Yet Theresa makes it a goal of hers to encourage and mentor Jane through the initial growing phase. Theresa's resilience, her perseverance, and her perception of her own abilities in relation to the situation help her keep her motivation and interest high.

Provide Social Role Models

When you see someone who is successful and has accomplished the same goal as you, even in the face of resistance, you are more apt to believe that you, too, can accomplish those same goals. You believe that you have the abilities to master the tasks required to reach your goals. This is why finding a role model or mentor who is similar to you can help build your self-efficacy. If you are leading a team or department, you can find social role models to encourage your employees to build their self-esteem.

Self-efficacy increases when you are able to relate to your role model or mentor.[8] If you surround yourself in cultural interactions with people who are not successful, even if you try very hard to be motivated in these challenges, this will undermine your efforts. Finding someone who has overcome cultural challenges will greatly benefit you. For example, read the following story about Tom, David, and Raj:

> Tom and David both lead sales departments for separate divisions of their manufacturing company. In the past 2 months, both have traveled frequently and separately to India to work with a new division of customer service representatives who work with their respective departments. Ever since their boss informed them of this new venture, Tom and David have had separate emotions and experiences related to the new business situation.
>
> Tom's been less enthusiastic and interested in the project. Having never been out of the country and working only nationally, he's hesitant and less thrilled than David about the new division and what it would entail. Similarly, David's never been out of the country, but he has, over time, cultivated interest in cultural experiences different from his own. He has intentionally taken part in different intercultural events at local and national levels. He can't wait to get started on the project.
>
> Raj, their division supervisor, knows the abilities of each member of her staff. She requires them to purchase books and resources to help them learn about the local Indian culture. She's even enrolled them in a language and culture class. She knows that Tom has been more reluctant to try new things. David seems

to be gaining momentum and retaining more of the information that he's learned compared to Tom. She notices the difference and thinks that Tom could learn from David.

Both have worked together closely in the past and share similar career and personal goals. Raj capitalizes on the relationship by building in a mentor-mentee component. She speaks to both of them about this new piece to their working relationship and receives an agreement and support from both. She also manages the relationship closely, ensuring that during this time Tom gets what he needs to be a culturally intelligent leader and that David receives mentorship and guidance from her. In this way, they're working as partners, each serving as role models and mentors to another person.

As a leader, Raj is able to identify intercultural competency areas where Tom and David can both benefit. Raj knows that Tom needs support to boost his confidence level when working across cultures. She also knows that David has the self-confidence but needs assistance in understanding cultural facts. By building strategies that are appropriate for each person, she builds her team's cultural intelligence. In the end, she learns about her own ability to work with two managers who have different individual cultural experiences.

Lead by Example

If you are able to manage and interact with different cultures more easily than your staff or employees are, model the way for them to understand how they could improve their own self-efficacies. Through your behaviors, your beliefs, and your thinking, you demonstrate, by example, the skills and knowledge they need to manage cultural environments. Jim Kouzes and Barry Posner,[9] in *The Leadership Challenge*, found that leaders should establish principles that guide people to reach their goals. Because a small shift or change could be overwhelming for some, helping them to set short, interim goals can help them to achieve larger goals. Modeling the way by identifying the barriers, being resourceful, and creating opportunities for your own success helps others to see their own abilities succeed. Take, for example, the case of Jaime and Anne:

Jaime is in her late 20s. She serves as the director of a civic engagement program in a nonprofit organization. Anne is in her late 50s and manages the program, reporting directly to Jaime. They've worked together for the past 3 years fairly well. They have their disagreements but overall have a healthy working relationship.

In the last year, the board of directors has changed the nature of the program to incorporate civic engagement and service learning principles. As a result, an increasing amount of volunteers in the program are college and high school students. Jamie notices that Anne has difficulty working with a younger generation of volunteers. She doesn't respond to them the way she responds to volunteers who are in her age group. Sometimes, Anne will make side comments about the younger generations' work ethics saying, "They're so unreliable" and "I don't know why they don't just pick up the phone to talk to me. It's like they don't know how to leave a message on voicemail anymore." She's even said these comments to her 55+ volunteers, who readily agree about the generational differences.

Jaime knows that Anne needs to be able to work with volunteers of all ages and cultural backgrounds. She's seen the negative impacts of Anne's behavior. Many of the younger volunteers come to Jamie if they have problems or issues when they should be going to Anne who directly manages them. They've expressed that Jaime is "more like them" and understands them. Although Jamie doesn't mind helping the volunteers with their questions, it's taking her away from her role and responsibilities as a leader of the department. Additionally, it's setting a tone for how Anne works and reshaping her job duties.

To resolve this, Jaime speaks with Anne about the issue. Anne doesn't see a problem with how she's handling the situation with younger volunteers. Jaime disagrees and at the end of the meeting, both agree to a plan that helps Anne to work more effectively with volunteers of any cultural background. Jamie and Anne work together to set goals that are achievable and work toward the long-term goals of the organization. Jaime finds opportunities to compliment Anne when she is successful and helps Anne to identify strategies that help her do her work more efficiently.

Jaime continues to work with Anne in the months to come. She's patient and believes that Anne will be able to adapt; however, after 2 years, Jaime decides to let Anne go because the situation does not change.

It is important to recognize that there are times that no matter how much you try to model the way for employees and others, it does not work out to the benefit of the organization. In the example of Jamie and Anne, after 2 years of Jaime modeling the way and helping Anne, the progress was not significant enough to make the change that was needed. There was still resistance on Anne's part. After much reflection and evaluation, Jaime decided to let Anne go. The cost of low self-efficacy affects not only Anne but also the program and the organization's overall goals.

Support Others in Their Self-Efficacy Development

As any leader should, it is important to support your staff, coworkers, and the organization to strengthen their self-efficacy. You can do this in several ways:

- Verbally tell them that they are making progress.
- Have evaluation or reflection sessions about the progress.
- Provide them with the right resources.
- Tell them to keep trying and to sustain their efforts.
- Know when to give feedback and what type of feedback to provide.

If you are looking to develop your own self-efficacy, then you need to put in systems that will help you. For example, find the role models and proper support mechanisms to ensure you do not fail. Finding support is important because your support system helps to minimize your attention on weaknesses; they provide constructive feedback to help you develop professionally.

Emphasize Self-Improvement

Unfamiliar cultural interactions are challenging, and you should look at your success and failures as personal and professional development. There will be times when you will be involved in cultural misunderstandings, make "cultural bloopers," or take part in a cultural conflict. This is just a part of the process of navigating through cultural terrain. When this happens, you need to focus on the value of self-improvement. Do not berate yourself over the mistake; learn to "learn and let go." When it is an employee who makes the mistake, do not compare them to others; rather, set a standard for improvement within cultural interactions and help the employee to get there. Notice how Jodi felt about herself in the following case study:

Jodi is a Magnetic Resonance Imaging (MRI) technician. She's been in the field for 10 years and works with a variety of patients from different cultural backgrounds. One day, an African woman, Aziza, her son, Guleed, and her husband, Hussein, comes into the clinic for an MRI. The son accompanies his parents and interprets as needed because, although they understand English, they have difficulty speaking it.

Jodi calls the patient to the MRI room. Her coworker, Melinda, assists her with the preparations and is with her in the room. Jodi prepares for the MRI by giving Aziza instructions, "You will lie down on the machine. You need to be very still or we have to start over." Jodi then turns to Guleed and speaks slowly, "Can you tell your mother that she needs to be very still when she's in there?"

Guleed understands and explains the MRI procedures to his mother. He then says to Jodi, "My mother has done this before. She had an MRI 3 years ago. She knows what to do."

"Okay," Jodi says. Again, her next instructions to Guleed are spoken in a slow pace, "Does she need medication to help her with staying still?"

Guleed shakes his head. "She's fine. She's done this before."

Jodi then turns to Aziza and says very slowly, "If you need help or to call us, you push this button." Her gestures to the family are overly emphasized when pointing to the call button. "Can you tell her to push this button if she needs help?" Guleed, looking more frustrated as the instructions are dictated, nods his head and explains to his mother.

After the MRI, Jodi courteously thanks the family and says, "You all did a very good job. Have a good rest of your day." The family quickly walks out and Guleed gives a slight smile in response.

Jodi and Melinda return to their work, and Jodi says "That family was interesting. It was so nice of that boy to come with his parents to interpret, don't you think?"

Melinda turns to Jodi and replies, "Yes, it was a good thing that he was there." She hesitates and then says, "But you know, you probably didn't need to talk like that to them."

With surprise, Jodi says, "Talk like what?"

"You were talking really slowly to them. It seemed like they didn't appreciate it. The son knew English very well and was fine interpreting and understanding what you told him."

Jodie replies, "Oh. But in that class we took the trainer said we should talk slow and not use big words so they can understand us. That's what I was doing. I mean, she probably didn't know what I was talking about so I had to talk slow to help her understand."

"Yeah, that's true but you were really dramatic about it. They're not deaf. They just have a harder time grasping the language."

Jodi pauses and then says, "You're right. How embarrassing! I hope they don't think badly of me. I was just trying to get them to understand what they needed to do. Next time I'll do it differently."

Jodi tries to apply what she has learned in cultural competency training, yet she is not able to apply the learning in a way that is appropriate to different racial and ethnic groups. This is evident when her colleague, Melinda, informs her that she thought Jodi used the wrong cultural competency tools. Jodi's instant emotional response was to be offended and to feel guilty for her intercultural mistakes. However, she realizes that her experience and mistake will only improve her ability to work better with different cultures.

Jodi can use the CI principles to help her in the following way:

- Acquire: In this case study, Jodi has good intentions to be respectful of another culture. But what she is not picking up on are the verbal and nonverbal cues of her environment. If Jodi can identify what she did well and where she could improve, she can better assess her level of understanding culture in this situation. Jodi has worked with families of different backgrounds, but it seems as if no one has told her that she was unintentionally creating an uncomfortable environment for those families. To acquire information about culture that can be helpful to her in future situations she can start with recognizing what cultural facts and knowledge she may already have. For example, she speaks slower to this family so they can understand. Yet she needs to know that not all families need to be spoken to in this manner.

- Build: If Jodi can take the knowledge she has, speaking slower in English can help those who are not English native speakers, and combine this with the knowledge that not all non-English speakers need to be spoken to in this way, then she will begin to build her awareness for when speaking slowly would be appropriate. When she does this, she is creating new information and making new sense of the cultural information.

- Contemplate: Even though Jodi is familiar working with families of different cultures, she can always approach the situations with new lenses or perspectives. By asking herself what she sees and does not see in the situation, she can shift her mindset from one that treats all families the same to one that treats them as unique. Contemplation requires Jodi to reflect on her biases as well as the unintentional consequences that come about because of her need to be culturally appropriate.

- Do: As she practices the strategies she creates for each family situation, she will learn what works and does not work for each family. She may even be surprised that she is adapting and changing her behaviors with every family she treats, even if the families share similar cultural backgrounds and interests. The more she practices and evaluates, the more she will reduce her need to be perfect in every cultural situation. Instead, she will learn that her mistakes become cultural lessons in practice.

Reduce Anxiety and Stress Related to Cultural Interactions

When we feel we are capable of accomplishing a goal, we have positive emotions. When we know that we do not have the abilities to accomplish the goal, our emotions and mood for the activity are less positive. How we feel can be a deterrent to our success by affecting our attitudes and perceptions of who we are and how we will achieve our goals. Our negative moods can create stress, anxiety, frustration, and fear—all which do not serve you in intercultural work. As a leader, you should help support strategies that reduce the stress and anxiety related to unfamiliar cultural situations. And if you are the one who gets anxious, stressed out, or disinterested, you should find strategies that work for you. The following are some tips for reducing stress and anxiety related to unfamiliar cultural settings that can bring about a more positive outlook:

- *Keep a stress journal.* Use the journal as a way to track your physical and emotional responses to unfamiliar cultural settings. As you write out your feelings, you will begin to see common themes and patterns in your behavior. When you can identify what makes you stressed and how you typically respond, you can find the appropriate strategies to reduce your stress level.

- *Keep a gratitude journal.* When we are stressed and our anxiety is high, we often cannot see the opportunities and positive outcomes in intercultural relationships. Keeping a gratitude journal enables us to identify the pieces of the relationship or the situation that contributes positively back to our self-development, even though, at the time, we may think it is the worst thing to have happened. Writing down a few things you are grateful for in the situation helps to shift your mind-set and calm your physical and emotional state.

- *Break your goal into smaller, manageable steps.* For example, if you need to learn a new language and culture but it seems overwhelming, break that goal into smaller tasks over time. Do not take on more than you can handle. If the time does not allow for it, ask your supervisor for support and ideas to make it more manageable.

- *Express your feelings and emotions in a healthy manner.* For example, you need to be able to communicate your feelings and thoughts to your supervisor. Your concerns should be expressed in a respectful manner. If you do not share your concerns with your supervisor, you will build resentment and emotional clutter around the situation. If this continues over time, you build unhealthy habitual patterns and responses every time you are in unfamiliar territory.

- *Be willing to compromise and let go.* Working with cultures means that you have to be adaptable and willing to let go of what you know. You have to be flexible or else you are always going to have problems that frustrate, disappoint, and anger you.

- *Stay calm and focused on the task.* The more anxious you are, the more you visualize and paint a picture that creates more stress for you. According to Bandura,[10] your stress level can impair how you function inter- and intrapersonally. Staying calm and focused helps you decrease your stress and anxiety.

- *Recognize that you cannot control culture.* Culturally intelligent leaders know that culture cannot be controlled. It is ever changing, never static. You have to recognize that there are times in cultural situations that you cannot anticipate, no matter how much you have trained, read resources, or lived in the culture. As in life, there are many things that are out of our control. We cannot expect that our intentions will always have the impact we envision it to be. This is why focusing on the things we can control, such as our adaptive responses to another person or culture, is better than stressing about what we cannot control.

- *Be willing to forgive.* People make mistakes. At times, people are not aware of what they have said or the implications of what they have done. When it comes to cultural intelligence, you have to be willing to forgive others both for what they are conscious and not conscious of doing, saying, or feeling. If you cannot forgive, you are going to have a hard time working with unfamiliar cultural environments.

- *Keep your sense of humor.* Working interculturally can be both tiring and exhilarating. There will be times when you make mistakes and feel disappointed for not picking up the cues or for not "knowing what to do." Keeping a sense of humor about culture lessens the stress. You have to be able to laugh at yourself; otherwise, the challenges of cultural differences become too much to bear.

I once consulted with an organization that had a tool called "The Wizard." This tool helped organizations to be more accountable and transparent in their use of charitable donations. They wanted to expand their tool to a diverse audience. In a session focused on thinking about how the tool could be more accessible, it struck us that, in one of the languages, the word "wizard" translated into "Shaman." In this community, the shaman happens to be someone who is wise and connects with the spirit world. Can you imagine going into the community and talking about how "the shaman" will help you to be more accountable? We all laughed, and we also used this as an opportunity to discuss the challenges of accessibility.

Chapter Summary

- Interactions within cultures are based on a person's sense of efficacy, which is their belief about their abilities to perform what is required in new cultural settings.
- Culturally intelligent leaders have higher levels of self-efficacy. They look at challenges as opportunities, they are resilient and persistent in their pursuance of the goal, they have higher confidence levels, and they are committed to finding solutions.
- Individuals who have low self-efficacy have lower expectations of themselves in new cultural settings, they lose interest and commitment under duress, and they focus on doubts and negative outcomes.
- Emotional intelligence speaks to the importance of self-efficacy in leadership; it points out the critical role self-efficacy has on managing one's emotions, adaptability, and optimism.
- Mindfulness brings about creativity and innovation. It takes leaders "out of their boxes" and gives them a new way of perceiving themselves, their abilities, and their world.
- Mindlessness comes about through repetitive behaviors. Mostly unconsciously, a state of mindlessness can lead to learned helplessness.
- Research has shown that you can improve your self-efficacy, and the chapter highlights areas for leadership development.

CHAPTER 6

Adapting and Performing

Early in my professional career, I was a part of a marketing and sales team that included two team members who had very different working styles and personalities. Louisa was quiet, spent a lot of time reflecting, and responded only when asked questions or prompted to speak. When she arrived at work, she went straight to her desk, shut the door, and got right to her tasks. She was seen as "level-headed," practical, and a no-nonsense type of person. When you had to ask her a question, you could find Louisa in her office, steadily working on her tasks and projects. When she spoke, she was direct and concise. Sometimes, when making a point or supporting argument, she numbered her points out loud, such as, "First, I think we need to do this. Second, we will move on to this. Third, if the previous situation does not work, then we can go to option two." Our team thought she was friendly, although a bit distant and not very personable in her interactions.

Joseph was the opposite. He was very gregarious in nature. He talked all the time, whether someone wanted to hear his ideas or not; most of the time, it was just entertaining to hear him speak and share his stories. After his arrival every morning, he went around to all the offices (this was a small organization) and chatted with whomever had arrived. It took him awhile to get settled into his office and to begin his work. When you needed Joseph to review a document or you needed to ask him a question, he could be found talking with people outside of his office. When he spoke, it was hard to follow his thoughts because he jumped from story to story, sometimes confusing himself in the process. And there were times that he would say things out loud, not to get our feedback but just to process the information. We thought he just liked hearing himself talk, and our team culture was such that we found him to be very personable and likeable, quirks and all.

As a young professional who was looking to make her mark on the working world, I found my time with Louisa to be extremely challenging. How was I to make an impression when this manager did not even want to talk to me? How was she to be aware of my talents and skill sets? I quickly learned that I related more easily to Joseph. He always asked me how I was, what projects I was working on, and whether I was enjoying my time with the organization. These conversations with Joseph were not short; rather, they often lasted as long as 30 minutes. Through these conversations, I learned a lot about the workings of the organization, where my skills could be most helpful, and where I could advance in the company.

Every time I interacted with Louisa, I took a cautious and pragmatic approach. I knew my conversations with her would be short and to the point. In the beginning, I went into her office, engaging her in dialogue about things outside of work and failed miserably. But after a few conversations, I picked up some verbal and nonverbal cues about her "conversation motto," which was "Make it short and to the point." I began to mimic her actions and language. When speaking about several points, I numbered them out loud the way she did. I found that I was more formal than usual with her than with others. I looked directly in her eyes and once even caught myself looking at my watch when I thought she was talking too long!

With Joseph, talking to him could take awhile. I talked to him only when I knew I had no other appointments or deadlines to meet. I entered his office with a singsong-like "hello," which was the way he greeted others. We never talked business right away. And I noticed that, when explaining a story or a point, my hand gestures always matched his. Even the tone of my voice mimicked his.

When I interacted with Louisa and Joseph, my behavior changed from person to person. I cannot tell you exactly when in our working relationship this began; I assume it happened partly on a conscious level and partly on a subconscious level. What is important to note about this personal story is that changing my behaviors enabled me to work better with both Louisa and Joseph.

Earley and Peterson stated, "Adopting the behaviors consistent with a target culture is an important aspect of intercultural adjustment and interaction."[1] Similarly, Thomas and Inkson said,

Whether or not social behavior takes place in a cross cultural setting, each situation will be unique and in particular will involve interaction with other unique people. . . . you must be able to adapt your general approach and specific interactions to the particular characteristics of the situation, and particularly, to the expectations of the other people involved.[2]

Thus, cultural intelligence requires that you engage in *adaptive behavior* and necessitates that you have the understanding and motivation to achieve it. This third element of cultural intelligence refers to the ability of individuals to go beyond thinking: they must be *doing* something. To be a culturally intelligent leader, it is not enough for you to know the information you need and how you will think about it, nor is it enough to be motivated. You must have the appropriate behavioral responses and be able to acquire or adapt the behaviors to new cultural situations. And you must be willing to try to learn new behaviors, and to know when and how to use them.

Learning new behaviors is considered the most challenging component of cultural intelligence. This is because behaviors are rooted in our beliefs and values. Rather than being skilled in particular sets of behaviors, as a culturally intelligent leader, it is better to have a repertoire of behaviors that you know of and use. You must be good at behaving in a manner that will not confuse other individuals. You cannot expect that your behavior will remain the same with all individuals from either the same or different cultural groups. You need to have a variety of behavioral skills you can draw from.

This chapter discusses four key ideas in relationship to adaptive behavior: the concept of self, cognitive dissonance, linguistic relativity, and behavior and communication.

Concept of Self

George Herbert Mead[3] argued that individuals develop a *self-concept* that evolves throughout their lives as a result of interacting with their social world, which may include parents, teachers, and peers. Similarly, William Purkey stated that "self-concept may be defined as the totality of a complex, organized, and dynamic system of learned beliefs, attitudes and opinions that each person holds to be true about his or her personal existence."[4] These interactions help individuals form a perception of who they are based on expectations from, and responses to, their social environment. Our perceptions are stimulated by internal and external factors. These factors can create intense emotional responses, which impact our willingness to learn and our choice of action—they guide individual behaviors. The following example demonstrates this idea of self-concept and how it manifests in one's behaviors.

Like many teenagers in the United States, Karen was required to take a foreign language course at her school. She chose to learn German because relatives on her mother's side lived in Germany, and her family was planning a visit in the summer. Unfortunately, Karen's few months of German class were not fun. She had a teacher who was very strict in her lesson plans and grading of the students. Additionally, Karen fell behind in the class work due to an afterschool sports injury; she was out for 2 weeks. When she returned to class, her teacher called her out in front of other students when she didn't know the correct vocabulary terms and proper responses. She didn't feel motivated to be in class and learn German.

When summer arrived, her family went to Germany as planned to visit their relatives. Karen's parents had been excited about her foreign language choice, and her relatives knew she was taking a German culture and language course. During the stay with her relatives, Karen tried to practice her German but stopped trying after her relatives told her, "You need to improve your German." The next year, her family visited Germany again, and her relatives questioned her about her German language skills. Upon hearing her speak, they told her again, "You're not there yet. You need a lot of improvements."

Twenty years later, Karen works for a financial company that has a location in Germany. Karen's supervisor tells her that she will need to relocate to Germany for 2 years; she thinks that with Karen's great interpersonal skills, she would be able to help the success of the project. Upon hearing this, Karen becomes anxious and uncomfortable. She makes excuses for not going, and her supervisor is confused. Karen has been an outstanding worker and her actions are puzzling and surprising.

Karen's self-concept has contributed to her self-efficacy. The expectations of her teacher, her family, and her relatives to learn a new language is too much for her to handle. The responses she receives are not what she wants or needs to hear to help her improve her German language skills. As a result, she withdraws from learning the language and culture. She develops a self-concept that may consist of any of the following:

- I will never learn the German language and culture.
- I do not have the ability or skills to learn a new language.
- It is easier if I just do what is comfortable for me.
- I cannot make mistakes or people will lose their confidence in me.

These beliefs and attitudes surface when her supervisor asks her to relocate to Germany. The negative memories and experiences she had become barriers to her success and self-efficacy. She feels anxious, and her behaviors are seen as strange.

Developing a Self-Concept

There are three general understandings about how a self-concept is developed. First, a **self-concept is learned**. As Mead indicates, a self-concept gradually emerges early in one's life and is constantly shaped throughout life by one's perceived experiences. This means that a self-concept is learned: it is a social product of one's experiences. The perception of one's self-concept may differ from how others perceive that person, and it is different during every life stage. When a person is presented with an experience that differs from the self-concept he or she has developed, the person sees the experience as a threat. The more experiences that challenge the self-concept, the more rigid the self-concept becomes. Generally, an individual will try to overthink, overgeneralize, or rationalize the experience so as to reduce the emotional havoc it creates.

Second, a **self-concept is organized**. Most scholars agree that individuals develop a self-concept that has stable characteristics in order to maintain harmony. Our self-concept is orderly: it categorizes our experiences and "fits" them in a way that will make sense to our development. It discards experiences that present different beliefs and values because it cannot be placed in a categorical way. It is our self-concept that tries to resist change, because the changes disrupt the stability of one's personality. Let us say you hold a very specific belief, such as, "English is the primary language of this country and everyone should learn to speak and write it. There is no reason to have billboards and signs in other languages." The more central this belief is to your self-concept, the more resistant you are to learning new experiences and to adapting your belief.

Third, a **self-concept is dynamic**. Self-concepts are actively shaped based on one's experiences, which means that they are dynamic. The self-concept can be seen as a guidance system directing your behaviors to match up with your beliefs. I often hear employees in organizations say, "My company does not do what it says it will do around diversity and inclusion. It says one thing, and its actions are completely the opposite." At an organizational level, the company may perceive itself differently, defending its self-concept. There is a conflict between this perception of who they are versus what others think they really are. Complaints from employees will be rationalized, or bended, to fit the self-concept of the organization and its leaders. In psychology, this is called cognitive dissonance, that is, one's justification for one's beliefs even when the facts clearly demonstrate the opposite.

The following case study illustrates the self-concept in action.

Joe leads a Public Safety department in Garden Grove, a suburb located just outside of a large urban city in the Midwest. He's lived and worked in this city all his life, and generations of his family have made Garden Grove their home. They settled in the area when it was just farmland and have seen it develop over time into a bustling city of 128,000.

Garden Grove, like other suburban cities in the United States, has seen an increase in the number of non-White residents. A large number of Asian residents move into the city because they are attracted to the educational system and quality of life the city offers. This change has made the city more racially diverse than ever.

Joe sees the visible differences on a personal and professional level. In his neighborhood, 25% of his neighbors are Asian Indian, 10% are Vietnamese, and 10% are Chinese. He's had problems with his neighbors; what used to be a quiet neighborhood is now a festival every week. His neighbors have lots of visitors who park up and down the side street, their children running around without any parental guidance. Once, he held a party to celebrate his son's graduation from high school, and his relatives and friends had to park two blocks away because of his neighbor's party.

At work, he's pressured from his director to hire more people who "reflect the community" that Garden Grove has become. From volunteers to paid staff, he's had to work through policy changes and make accommodations for who he hires. He disagrees with his director that he should hire someone just to make a quota, and besides, he can't find anyone who has the skills or the experience for the department jobs. Although he loves his job, it's not what it used to be. He's increasingly unmotivated to go to work. It seems that all he does these days is attend training sessions on diversity. What's happened to his passion for public service?

As the director, you have noticed the changes in Joe. You know it has to do with the new vision of the organization to increase racial and cultural diversity as part of the city's strategic vision. To help Joe manage his self-concept, think about the following questions: What do you think is Joe's self-concept? What are the beliefs that are being challenged? When evaluating this case study, there are several items that are important to note:

- Joe has a long history of family traditions and roots in Garden Grove.
- His experiences and knowledge of Garden Grove span generations.
- Joe and his family are accustomed to interacting with people who are Caucasian.
- He has a belief that his neighborhood was a "quiet" place to live, but it is now disrupted because of the new neighbors, who are not so quiet.

- He has a belief that the parties thrown by his neighbors are so large that he considers them festivals.
- He does not understand the collective nature of the Asian Indians, Vietnamese, and Chinese neighbors in his neighborhood.
- He believes that one should be hired on the basis of merit and skill rather than filling a quota.

All of these items are some examples of Joe's beliefs that form his self-concept. In the case study, you can also identify what emotions and feelings he has related to his self-concept, such as his discomfort with non-Whites. Identifying emotions is useful for understanding how the self-concept develops to make the person feel comfortable.

Developing a Self-Understanding

One's self-concept is developed throughout one's lifetime and has an impact on behaviors and choice of action. How have you come to understand yourself over time? How has this understanding led to the choices you make? One way of gaining knowledge of who you are is through personality assessments. There is a plethora of assessments and inventories, and I describe three that I have used successfully with diverse audiences. I have found that these three assessments are excellent tools for building cultural intelligence and leadership.

- *Reflected "Best Self" Exercise* helps individuals to identify their strengths and talents. The exercise requires that you seek out and request feedback from significant people in your life—siblings, parents, friends, coworkers, colleagues, mentors, supervisors, relatives, and so on. Once you collect the information, you create a picture of your "best self."[5]
- *Via Institute on Character* is a nonprofit organization that was founded in 2000 by Dr. Martin E. P. Seligman and Dr. Neal H. Mayerson. The organization provides, free of charge, a survey (VIA Survey of Character) that measures 24 character strengths. VIA stands for "Values in Action," and the survey can be used to help improve one's performance and well-being.[6]

- *The Enneagram Institute* provides a personality assessment to help you discover and understand your personality type. The institute suggests that there are nine basic personality types, and these types serve as a framework for understanding oneself and working with others.[7]

Cognitive Dissonance

Parker Palmer wrote, "When leaders operate with a deep, unexamined insecurity about their own identity, they create institutional settings that deprive *other* people of *their* identity as a way of dealing with the unexamined fears in the leaders themselves."[8] What Palmer speaks to is a level of dissonance that often occurs in human interactions, particularly with leaders.

Cognitive dissonance is a state of discomfort that humans experience when one of their beliefs, ideas, or attitudes is contradicted by evidence or when two of their beliefs, ideas, or attitudes come into conflict with each other. Dissonance makes people feel uncomfortable and "is bothersome under any circumstance, but it is most painful to people when an important element of their self-concept is threatened—typically when they do something that is inconsistent with their view of themselves."[9] A famous case in cognitive dissonance comes from the work of Leon Festinger, who described the workings of cognitive dissonance that occurred in a group setting.

Festinger and his associates studied a group that believed that the earth was going to be destroyed by a flood on a certain date. This belief led group members to gather in the same location and pray; by doing so, they believed they would be saved. In the end, there was no flood and no end of the world. So what happened to the members? For the group members who were really committed to the belief (basically, giving up their homes and jobs), when the flood did not happen, these individuals had a large dissonance between their beliefs and the evidence they saw. Because of this large gap between their beliefs and the evidence at hand, they were more likely to reinterpret the evidence to show that they were right all along. For example, they would say that the earth was not destroyed because they came together to pray.

While these individuals justified their beliefs, the others recognized the foolishness of the experience and changed their beliefs or actions.

Using this example to guide our thinking about cultural intelligence, we can see that culturally intelligent leaders must be able to address the dissonance between their beliefs, ideas, or attitudes and behaviors. When leaders fail to see the connection, they are not really walking the cultural intelligence they talk. Some leaders will justify their beliefs even when the evidence eventually contradicts their belief systems. And rarely do we see organizational leaders change their beliefs or actions to align with what they say they will do around diversity and culture.

Learning and Dissonance

Dissonance can also occur when new learning or ideas are presented that conflict with what is already known. For example, an employee is required to attend a diversity workshop. During the session, the employee hears ideas that contradict, or come in conflict with, her belief about the topic. This employee already has certain knowledge about cultural diversity that she brings to the workshop, and because she is especially committed to her own knowledge and belief system, it is more likely that the employee will resist the new learning.

You can tell when a person is struggling with dissonance when you hear statements like, "Why can't people who come to this country be more like us," or "Why do we have to take these classes," or "I have to change my belief (or what I do) just to accommodate someone else?" More often than not, when the new learning is difficult, uncomfortable, or even humiliating, people are more likely to say that the learning or workshop was useless, pointless, or valueless. To admit one's dissonance would symbolize that one has been "had" or "conned" into believing something different.

If all this sounds familiar to you, or resonates with what is going on in your organization, you are not alone. Our behaviors are very much rooted in beliefs that are not completely explored within a working environment. Organizational leaders do not clearly articulate how to think about and practice cultural intelligence. The result is a failure to implement and practice cultural intelligence that corresponds with the belief systems. Organizational leaders—especially those specifically working on diversity initiatives—need to identify the points of dissonance that occur in their organization and among their staff. Leaders should pay attention to this dissonance and how it is being expressed.

Larger Gaps, Larger Dissonance

According to cognitive dissonance theory, the more important the issue and the larger the gap between the beliefs, the greater the dissonance among people. This is critical for leaders to understand because culture is a very important issue within an organization. There are inherently large gaps in beliefs on a personal, team, and organizational level related to this culture. Individual beliefs about power and privilege—as they relate to gender inequity, race inequity, generational differences, ability and disability, sexual orientation, religion, and so on—need to be explored in organizations and among leaders. If dissonance is not discussed, leaders will continue to employ workers who (a) feel uncomfortable talking about culture and diversity, (b) continue to behave in inappropriate ways, (c) are accepting of culture on the outside but do not align diversity with their beliefs, and (d) feel that all they need are the "right tools" or the "right answers" to be culturally competent.

Without careful attention to exploring the stories of dissonance, leaders allow their organizations to bury their inclusion blind spots. Blind spots in cognitive dissonance describe the things you cannot see because they are hidden or because you choose not to see them. We are unaware of our blind spots because our focus is directed toward other things or we are distracted from what needs to be done. Blind spots can lead to underestimating or overestimating our cultural abilities and to truly understanding what needs to be done regarding culture and diversity. Regardless of the talent that is recruited, the accomplishments or progress that is made, or even how much money is poured into diversity initiatives, these blind spots can cause leaders to miss opportunities that bring about positive, transformative change and innovation.

Given this information, what can leaders do about the cultural dissonance within their organizations? First, leaders must have the courage to be open to the possibilities that their beliefs, or the organization's beliefs, are not aligned with their actions and behaviors. It takes courageous leadership to *not* maintain the status quo and to explore the stories that give root to organizational and individual beliefs. Second, leaders can, and should, explore the dissonance by asking themselves the following questions:

- What are my organization's beliefs about culture?
- What dissonance is present in our beliefs and our behaviors?
- What gaps (in recruitment, within policy, and in intrapersonal interactions) are created because of the dissonance?
- How is this dissonance stopping us from truly understanding culture?

In cultural intelligence work, it is critical that you recognize your self-concept to understand your blind spots. As a leader, it is your responsibility to help others recognize their self-concept and the role it plays in intercultural interactions. It is essential for you to understand that people will often choose to stick to their beliefs (even if it no longer serves them) to alleviate the emotional stress that reorganizing a self-concept requires. They would rather fend off the perceived threat than create learning opportunities out of these experiences.

Finally, it is important for leaders to work with employees to explore employee dissonance. Learning to work with, and understand, cultures is not the sole responsibility of leaders; it is the responsibility of everyone within an organization. Because leaders are in the positional power to promote and support the work, it is the responsibility of the leaders to help their employees uncover their blind spots. With clear sight of these blinds spots, organizations can turn them into an advantage. By doing so, organizations can find significantly greater possibilities that expand and deepen intercultural work than previously imagined.

Adapting and Modifying Behaviors

When we learn something new, we change our perspectives of our world, the way we interact with others, and our behaviors. We also learn when our behaviors are inappropriate and, hopefully, learn not to repeat them. We do this by adjusting our behaviors so that the situation does not occur again. We act differently based on previous consequences. If our behaviors resulted in a positive impact, we would continue the behavior. Take, for example, the following story about New Zealand's soccer team, "All Whites."

After landing from a long flight from Austria, New Zealand's soccer team, *All Whites*, heads to the South African stadium for their first day of training. They are met by a "smelly fog" on the field, making it difficult for players and coaches to breathe and see. One player comments on the smell and smog saying, "You could tell [it was smoky] as we came in on the bus. You could taste it, breathe it on the bus. It's something that's a bit different for us and something else to adapt to on tour." The management team debates canceling the training and in the end decides to have players stretch their legs and get some exercise. Local South Africans on staff are confused at the entire ruckus and can't understand why a team would stop playing because of a "little smog." The players and team management can't understand how anyone could play under such conditions.[10]

Learning a new pattern of behavior requires modifying small behaviors that add up to a complex behavior. Learning new patterns can be difficult but the motivation to modify and change can be transformational. Kevin Cashman said that positive change means letting go of our old behaviors and allowing change to be our teacher.[11] As leaders, we must recognize our own capacity to change—that we have what it takes to make a change. To make a change, you need to believe you are capable of performing the behavioral change and that there is an incentive to change. Similarly, Margaret Wheatley said this about the human capacity to change and transform,

> Viability and resiliency of a self-organizing system comes from its great capacity to adapt as needed, to create structures that fit the moment. Neither form nor function alone dictates how the system is organized. . . . The system may maintain itself in its present form or evolve into a new order, depending on what is required. It is not locked into any one structure; it is capable of organizing into whatever form it determines best suits the present situation.[12]

When making changes to your behaviors, there are three questions to ask to help initiate the change. [13]

What is changing? To understand change, you must be clear about what you want to change in your cultural interactions. Then, make it your intention to change and carry out the change. Finally, your change must be linked to your motivation for changing. You will need to ask, Why is it important that I make this change? How will this change my future interactions with this individual or cultural group?

What will actually be different because of the change? Because transformative change in cultural interactions can be hard, the ability to visualize the end result or outcome of the change can help move the situation forward. Visualization requires an articulation for what the desired result and outcomes look like. Setting clear expectations for getting to the desired result can help motivate you to making the change.

Who's going to lose what? In any cultural shift you will need to ask yourself, What beliefs and values might I have to let go? Why is it hard to abandon your beliefs and values? How well have these values and beliefs served you? What are the barriers they create for your future? Consider the following case study of two individuals' behaviors in relation to one other:

> Jose is from Costa Rica and Mary is from Great Britain. They work together in an international company located in the United States. Mary notices that whenever Jose talks, he always inches closer to her personal space. She's extremely uncomfortable when this happens and always takes steps back to give more physical space to the conversation. When she does this, Jose comes closer. One time, Mary was backed up to a work place counter and Jose didn't even notice!

Imagine that Mary and Jose work for you, and Mary has approached you with her concerns. To help Mary find a solution to this situation, use Table 6.1 to help you to think through some important questions; then, look at the second column as one possible perspective or thought about the question. Finally, fill in your perspective and thoughts.

Self-concept does not necessarily mean that you have the knowledge and skills to be where you need to be. Because change and transitions are emotionally and psychologically taxing, making a connection between the behavior change and the outcomes can help to ease the transition.

Table 6.1. Changing Cultural Behaviors

Questions	One Perspective/Thoughts	Your Perspective/Thoughts
How do Mary and Jose view personal space? How does this impact their behaviors?	Mary feels a great need for personal space. As a woman, perhaps she feels a greater need for this space. Jose does not see a problem with the personal space. Maybe getting closer to her is one way of relating to her.	
What are the adaptive behaviors needed in this situation?	Mary and Jose need to understand that everyone has different ideas of what personal space means. It may be helpful for Mary and Jose to talk about personal space issues, especially what it looks like for both of them. Perhaps Mary is the only person who feels uncomfortable and the only one to have brought this up. Maybe others do not feel the same way.	
What, if anything, will Mary and Jose lose if they change their behaviors?	Through conversation, Jose and Mary will discover that their idea of personal space is related to their cultural upbringing. They might be resistant to the change in the beginning, because they see it as "their individual cultures or their national cultures."	
What will be gained from changing the behaviors of Mary and Jose?	Mary and Jose will have a greater understanding for working together. Mary can focus on what Jose says instead of focusing on his body language toward her, and Jose can learn to control his own body language and to read that of others.	

In some cases, if an individual is not responding to the change, rewards and reinforcers are used to increase a behavioral response. Even adding a compliment can increase a person's behavior. However, if a person does not know what fuels his or her self-concept, then the challenge in making a transition will be more difficult.

Linguistic Relativity

In *The Spirit Catches You and You Fall Down*, Anne Fadiman[14] described the story of a Hmong refugee family, the Lees, and their intercultural interactions with doctors in Merced, California. The story is about Lia Lee, the second-youngest daughter, who is diagnosed with severe epilepsy. Within the Hmong culture, epilepsy is not described in the same way that Western medical doctors describe it; epilepsy is described as *qaug dab peg* or "the spirit catches you and you fall down." According to animism, the foundation for Hmong religious beliefs, both good and bad spirits surround us. Epileptic attacks are seen as the ability of an individual to temporarily join the spirit world. This is seen as honorable because the spirits have chosen that person to communicate with them.

The language used by Hmong and Americans to describe their understanding and knowledge of what was happening to Lia can be referred to as linguistic relativity. Linguistic relativity was first developed by Edward Sapir and Benjamin Lee Whorf and is known as the Sapir-Whorf hypothesis,[15] or the *principle of linguistic relativity*. It describes the idea that language influences the perceptions and thoughts of people, thus affecting their behavior. In Hmong culture, there is no word for "*epilepsy*"; instead, the word is associated with the animistic worldview of the Hmong, which serves as a philosophical, religious, and spiritual guide to operating one's life. The only way to describe epilepsy is related to this world view of spirits. In Western medicine and science, rationality, logic, and objectivity are important—scientific words and definitions are not abstract; rather, they are concrete.

Sapir and Whorf argued that individuals are not aware of the influence of language, and it is only when moving between cultures that individuals become aware. A commonly cited example of linguistic relativity is the example of how Inuit Eskimos describe snow. In English, there is only one word for snow, but in the Inuit language, many words are used to describe snow: "wet snow," "clinging snow," "frosty snow," and so on.

The following case study further explains the idea behind linguistic relativity:

> Carol serves as a program director for a local nonprofit in the Washington DC area. Her organization has received a federal grant to implement employment training and resources to serve the large and growing Somali population in the area. The grant requires her organization to track the outcomes and impact of the training program on participants' lives. Each participant is required to attend an exit interview session conducted by a staff person.
>
> Carol creates a survey that is both qualitative and quantitative to measure the impact. Questions relate to the participant's experience in the program and ask participants to rate their level of agreement to statements. Table 6.2 shows sample questions from the quantitative survey.
>
> Pattie serves as the interviewer for all the sessions. She reads out loud each statement and given the responses, checks the appropriate box. She notices that during the first round of interviews, participants are unsure how to respond. They are unclear about the levels of rating given to them: *strongly agree, agree, disagree,* and *strongly disagree.* Additionally, some of the statements

Table 6.2. Survey to Measure Program Impact

Statements	Strongly Disagree	Disagree	Agree	Strongly Agree
I know how to use the Internet to find a job.				
I am able to put together a resume for a job.				
When I find a job I like, I know how to respond to the job posting.				
I know the appropriate questions to ask a potential employer in interviews.				

are confusing. She tries to explain the difference but is unsure how to describe the statements differently. She's frustrated because she's concerned she's not getting the right information, and she knows that it must upset the participants.

Carol and Pattie discuss what they could do differently in the survey or process to help the Somali participants understand the questions. Unfortunately, they do not have an employee on staff that can translate. In the end, Carol and Pattie decide to change the process and the language barriers in the interview. They decide that pictures may help illustrate a level of agreement. They also agree to take out the "big words" or words that would further confuse the participants. They also changed the rating scale to reflect: *yes, no, and maybe*. The revised survey had the following questions.

I know how to use the Internet to find a job.
I know how to create a resume for a job.
When I find a job I like, I know who to call in the company.
I know what I can and can't ask in interviews.

Now imagine that you are Carol's boss and you have been updated about this situation. What suggestions do you have for Carol and Pattie as they continue their work?

There are a number of ways to think about the work. In cultural intelligence, understanding how to adapt your behavior is critical. The following are questions that you should think about in order to help Carol and Pattie adapt their behaviors:

- What emotions come up for you in this work?
- Are the emotions negative or positive? How does it fuel your work?
- What is the influence of language on evaluation?
- What body language do you notice? What does it tell you? How can it be helpful to our work to identify verbal and nonverbal cues?
- What are we doing that works?
- What do we know does not work in this project?
- What are the learning opportunities for all?

Asking these questions is a start toward continuing the good work that Carol and Pattie have already begun. As the two move forward in their work and learn more about what works and what does not work, they will learn to ask and reflect on questions that are inclusive to other cultures.

Behavior and Communication

Our behaviors are communicated both verbally and nonverbally. Culturally intelligent leaders pay attention to both cues. Earley et al.[16] noted, "When we meet strangers from other cultures for the first time, their outward appearances and overt behaviors are the most immediately obvious features, not their hidden thoughts and feelings." I experienced this when on my first trip from the United States to France.

In my mid-20s, I went to France with my family to visit my uncle on my mother's side. As we boarded the flight and found our seats, my father and I had challenges finding an overhead space for our bags. Because we did not want to hold up the line of people who needed to pass us to get to their seats, we needed some assistance. I explained to my father in our native Hmong language that there were flight attendants who could assist us. Not too far from us, I spotted a flight attendant and said to my father, "I think he could help us."

My father, who was distracted and gently being pushed to the side by much taller passengers making their way to their seats, could not see where the attendant was. I said, while pointing in the direction of the attendant, "Dad, he's over there." My father looked up and, at that same time, I looked over at the flight attendant. We made eye contact, and because the plane was bustling with passengers, rather than calling out for assistance, I signaled with my hands for him to come over to us.

The next thing I knew, the flight attendant came over. I was so ecstatic to see that he was going to help us that what he said took me by surprise. "In our country, we don't point our fingers at other people. It's rude." Because his voice was loud, other passengers turned to look at what was going on. Completely embarrassed, I said, "I'm sorry. I didn't know." He replied curtly, "Don't ever do this [points his finger at me] again."

"Okay. Thanks for letting me know," I responded with an apologetic tone. It was certainly not my intention to point directly at him, or to call him to us in that manner.

After settling in our seats with the plane on its way to France, I found myself getting emotional about the situation. *He thinks I'm rude for pointing? He's rude for not even letting me explain. Besides, I didn't point my finger at him. I was just pointing in the direction he was standing. And, what's his problem that he doesn't know pointing fingers is also rude in America? Does he think I'm NOT from America?*

I describe the emotions I felt as my "emotional hijack" moment, which is when the thalamus in the brain bypasses the "thinking brain" (cortex) and sends signals directly to the amygdala (emotional brain); I took out my journal and deconstructed the situation. It was my way to slow down and understand what happened; it was an opportunity to think through my thinking.

From this experience, I was reminded of the impact verbal and non-verbal communication has within intercultural interactions. And sometimes, the intention of your communication does not have the impact that you hoped for.

Silence

Edward Hall[17] found that silence serves as a critical communication device and that it is viewed differently in different cultural contexts; he called these cultural contexts high-context and low-context cultures. Societies around the world fall into one or the other cultural context. Hall explained that in high-context cultures, pauses and silence reflect the thoughts of the speaker whereas, in many European countries, silence can be uncomfortable. Aida Hurtado[18] found that women of color used *silence and outspokenness* as a mechanism of testing knowledge and acquiring new knowledge about social environments. She argued that women of color use silence as a strategy for obtaining and reconstructing knowledge, and the usage of *outspokenness* compliments silence in that "knowing when to talk and just exactly what to say is especially effective if individuals are not expected to talk."[19]

As culturally intelligent leaders, we have to recognize the moments of silence and their meaning. As an educator in the United States, I often come across students in my classroom and training who are from high-context cultures. The majority of them do not speak unless specifically called out to provide a response; this differs from my students who are from low-context cultures, such as the United States, who constantly raise their hands and have something to say. The following is another example of silence and talk:

> A few years ago, Dr. Osmo Wiio, a communication scholar from Finland came to the United States as a visiting professor. While riding a public bus to the campus, a woman sitting next to him struck up a conversation, intending to be friendly. "I see by your clothes that you may be a European. What country are you from?" Wiio replied curtly, trying to discourage further conversation: "Finland." He held his newspaper so as to cover his face. But his fellow passenger stated, "Oh, how wonderful! Please tell me all about Finland." Professor Wiio felt very angry that a complete stranger had initiated a conversation with him. In Finland, a cultural norm discourages striking up conversation with strangers in public places.[20]

Cultural norms can also vary within a country. In some parts of the United States, a stranger attempting to initiate a conversation would be treated brusquely, while in other parts of the country, the same stranger would be treated kindly.

Self-Disclosure

Individual behaviors also differ based on a culture's notion of self-disclosure, the degree to which individuals share personal information with others. In general, collectivist and high-context cultures do not disclose much, while individualistic and low-context cultures are more self-disclosing. Take, for example, the following case study of a market research company that conducted surveys for their client, a health clinic:

> ActiveSearch, a market research company in the Midwest, was contracted to conduct follow up surveys with patients of a local health clinic. The clinic wanted to improve the quality of services and care provided and especially wanted to receive feedback from their African, Southeast Asian, and Latino patients. The phone surveys were short, no more than 10 questions that asked about

the quality of service, reason(s) for visit, timeliness, and ability of staff to respond knowledgeably and appropriately. Phone surveyors made calls to 1000 patients who were seen by the clinic within a 6-month period. To the surprise of the market research company, they encountered what they perceived in the beginning as "resistance" to respond to the satisfaction survey. Results from the surveys were disappointing because fewer than 70 African, Latino, and Southeast Asians participated compared to 638 White patients who responded. After careful evaluation and reflection, the company realized their error. African, Latino, and Southeast Asians patients did not want to share their health concerns with the surveyors; they were suspicious of the company. Whereas, White patients were accustomed to taking satisfaction surveys and did not express concerns over how the information would be used.

ActiveSearch mistook the refusal to participate as "resistance." The company did not realize that the African, Latino, and Southeast Asian groups they surveyed had cultural norms that spoke to keeping information within certain circles. The idea of sharing one's health issues is considered a private family matter in these groups, and trust was a large issue as well, as they were not sure what the information would be used for. Many respondents may even have thought they would lose their insurance or health care if they gave out information. Understanding the different belief systems that underline the cultural norms of self-disclosure would have been helpful to the business.

Maintaining Relationships

In their communication behaviors, collectivist cultures emphasize the importance of maintaining relationships. They will shape messages that will not be offensive, shaming, or cause a person to lose face. To a person from an individualistic culture, however, the message may be unclear, indirect, and ambiguous. The following case study provides an example of this:

Savitha and Mary are new coworkers who have worked together for the past 6 months. Mary feels that she would like to get to know Savitha better. She invites Savitha and other colleagues to a barbeque at her house. Savitha declines, saying, "Thank you but I have a family commitment that day." Mary understands and says, "Of course. Hopefully we can do something another time." Over the next year, Mary invites Savitha on several occasions to join her for coffee, dinner, or social events—sometimes with colleagues and sometimes just the two of them. Each time that Mary suggests a time to get together, Savitha responds that she is busy. Savitha says "no" because she also believes that her relationship with Mary needs to stay at a professional level, but she doesn't tell this to Mary. Mary's beginning to think that Savitha does not like her, and if that's the case, why doesn't she just come right out and say that?

In this example, Savitha is maintaining what she perceives as a harmonious relationship with her family, which Mary does not understand. From a collectivist culture, Savitha wants to ensure that the family relationship dynamics are not disturbed. Additionally, she wants to preserve the harmony of a professional relationship with Mary; rather than disrupt the flow of that relationship, she chooses to communicate this indirectly to Mary. She does not want Mary to lose face or take offense, yet the results are exactly the opposite of what Savitha expects. Mary thinks she is evasive. Both Savitha and Mary can learn about the different ways that different cultures express relationships and maintain healthy relationships. If both were aware of each other's cultural norms, they could adapt their behaviors.

The Concept of Face

An important aspect of interpersonal relationships is the concept of *face*. "Face" is seen as one's public image in social contexts, and this concept is very important in Asian cultures that have a collectivist identity. These societies are concerned with *saving face*, or how they will appear to those around them. Public criticisms that can lead to a person *losing face* may harm the person's identity and image, especially within their families and communities. Losing face can lead to deadly consequences, as in the following example:

In August 2007, Mattel was forced to recall over 900,000 plastic toys due to excessive amounts of lead in the paint. Later that month, Zhang Shuhong, the CEO of Lee Der Industrial in China, the manufacturer of the toys, committed suicide after China temporarily banned the company's exports. A Chinese newspaper said that a supplier, Zhang's best friend, sold Lee Der fake paint that was used in the toys. "The boss and the company were harmed by the paint supplier, the closest friend of our boss," the report said. It continued that "in China it is not unusual for disgraced officials to commit suicide."

Later that year, in September, Mattel's Executive Vice President for Worldwide Operations, Thomas Debrowski made a public apology to the Chinese government saying, "Mattel takes full responsibility for these recalls and apologizes personally to you, the Chinese people and all of our customers who received the toys. It is important for everyone to understand that the vast majority of these products that we recalled were the result of a flaw in Mattel's design, not through a manufacturing flaw in Chinese manufacturers."[21]

As this case illustrates, this situation even led to Mattel trying to save its face with the Chinese government and its people.

Time

Time is an important value dimension of culture and, as a result, impacts the behaviors of people. As discussed in chapter 2, time is regarded in some cultures as punctuality, while, in others, time is more relaxed and is viewed as contributing to the building of relationships. The following case study illustrates the notion of time and the behaviors of cultures based on their interpretations of time.

Tim, a White man, manages a production department in an American private business. Many of his assembly line workers come from the Southeast Asian and Asian cultures. Whenever his employees had a problem, they would want to talk and discuss the project at length. They not only wanted to understand the problem, but they wanted to keep harmony in the organization. They would come back to him several times even after the problem was resolved. For this manager, the problem had a quick solution: he provides the solution and his employees should comply. However, he doesn't understand why his employees keep coming back to him about the issues. He's annoyed at the amount of time it is taking to manage the process.

Tim and his employees have been raised with different notions of time. Tim thinks that time is associated with efficiency and effectiveness. To him, when an issue is discussed and a solution is provided, he believes there should be no further discussion. For his employees, the act of coming back to the problem is not to find more solutions; rather, it is to continue to develop a relationship with the manager—it is to ensure that the relationship is harmonious and in balance. For them, it is a check-in point in the relationship.

LeBaron[22] noted that cultural understanding of time can impact conflict management and negotiation processes. As an example, she described a negotiation process between First Nations people and the local Canadian government. She wrote,

First Nations people met with representatives from local, regional, and national governments to introduce themselves and begin their work. During this first meeting, First Nations people took time to tell the stories of their people and their relationships to the land over the past seven generations. They spoke of the spirit of the land, the kinds of things their people have traditionally done on the land, and their sacred connection to it. They spoke in circular ways, weaving themes, feelings, ideas, and experiences together as they remembered seven generations into the past and projected seven generations forward.

When it was the government representatives' chance to speak, they projected flow charts showing internal processes for decision-making and spoke in present-focused ways about their intentions for entering the negotiation process. The flow charts were linear and spare in their lack of narrative, arising from the bureaucratic culture from which the government representatives came. Two different conceptions of time: in one, time stretches, loops forward and back, past and future are both present in this time. In the other, time begins with the present moment and extends into the horizon in which the matters at hand will be decided.[23]

You can probably guess the result of this meeting. Both sides felt misunderstood and neither was happy with the results. Their world views, including the language used in the negotiation processes, originated from separate paradigms. Because neither of the groups understood the dimension of time and the influence of language in their behaviors, it led to decreased trust between them.

Changing Behaviors, Changing Minds

Successful adaptation requires cultural strategic thinking, motivation, and mindfulness. In this way, cultural intelligence principles are interconnected and interrelated. You must be able to think about your thinking, contemplate it, and then adapt it based on your findings and reflections. Behaviors, whether appropriate or inappropriate, must be identified and defined in objective terms. You have to know exactly what behaviors are reoccurring and why they need to be changed. By doing so, you can describe the things you say to yourself as well as the situations or behaviors that you are imagining. You can, and should, talk about the evaluation statements you make about yourself. The use of cultural strategic thinking and mindfulness can help you to identify your behaviors and thought patterns.

Table 6.3 is a case study of Gillian, who has been asked by her supervisor to lead development for a new service in her organization. Observe how she analyzes the situation in order to identify her behavior, the thoughts she had, and the emotions or behavioral outcomes she experienced.

Next, Gillian decides to find a way to manage her distressing thoughts and emotions. Because her anxiety, fear, and nervousness do not serve her as a leader in this work, she needs to identify more desirable thoughts. When she does this, she is less likely to have negative emotional responses that can lead to depressed moods and behaviors. To reframe her behavior, she will ask three questions:

Table 6.3. Identifying Behaviors and Thought Patterns

Situation	Thoughts	Emotions or Behaviors
My manager placed me in a work group to lead development for a new service in our organization. Working with the team requires that I make several trips to different parts of the world to speak with different team members. I have never worked with any of the individuals before and have not worked in a multicultural team.	I don't know if my responses and interactions with them will be appropriate. I don't know what to expect because we are a new team. I'm not even sure I know how they want to interact with me. Do they think I will be controlling, demanding? Should I be more participatory than usual in my leadership style? I don't want to mess this up.	I feel anxious. I am not as confident in myself and my abilities. I feel nervous about the whole thing. I feel like I'm losing control.

Where is the evidence that contributes to my thoughts? Gillian will use this broader question to further explore her confidence, her ability to manage the team, and whether she has facts that support her thought pattern

Are there other possibilities to this situation? Gillian will use this broader question to explore what she is not seeing in the situation and whether the facts presented are true or if there are other explanations.

What are the implications of my behaviors? Gillian will use this broader question to understand how she feels, whether the feelings help or hinder her, if the feelings create a positive end result, and what consequences would occur because of her resistance to change.

When Gillian is able to identify the negative or inappropriate behaviors and identify the behaviors she wants, she is then able to respond and adapt appropriately. Sometimes during the adaptation and adjustment period, it is helpful to recite self-statements to cue you in the direction of the positive behaviors you want to express. Peer support can also be helpful in changing minds because your peers can help point out in the situations where you revert back to old behaviors.

Changing Minds Through Storytelling

Gardner wrote in *Changing Minds* that to "capture the attention of a disparate population: create a compelling story, embodying that story in one's own life, and presenting the story in many different formats so that it can eventually topple the counterstories in one's culture."[24] Stories can, and do, shape culture in positive and negative ways. They help shape processes such as orienting new employees, they can serve as symbols that reinforce norms such as cubicles for employees and suites for executives, or they can create organizational heroes and heroines such as employee stories of leaders that go the extra mile.

Storytelling is an excellent way for leaders to garner staff involvement, bring new clients to an organization, or paint a vision of an organization's future. In its essence, storytelling is about how you communicate your vision, your goal, or your objective to listeners—in other words, storytelling can help you get your point across. Telling different stories can initiate different actions from story listeners, eliciting stories that speak to their behaviors and their experiences.

The impact of storytelling in organizations has become increasingly important because stories are memorable, no matter how poorly or well told they are. Emerging research studies show that storytelling has a tremendous effect on an organization's capacity to grow and manage change. Organizations in transition that use elements of storytelling demonstrated improvements in team performance and in overall project management. Although the research literature on storytelling is limited, the importance of storytelling is being noted on an international level. Stories, like Gardner expressed, are powerful tools, and when the right story is told, leaders can take the proper action needed for intercultural work.

Storytelling Unites Cultures

Storytelling is a unique strategy for socializing members into your organization and encouraging them to abide by cultural norms and values. This technique is especially helpful in guiding new members in understanding company values and beliefs. New employees will have assumptions about what to expect in their first day on the job. They often create their own realities, through their own stories, of what the organization is to them based on the behaviors, actions, and attitudes seen, heard, or felt during this initial phase. For current employees, storytelling emphasizes the important aspects of an organization's culture that you want them to value and demonstrate in their work. Perhaps these aspects have been previously missing from the organization, and by using storytelling techniques, you automatically bring people together by creating and sharing a common story.

As leaders, it is important to cultivate stories that have meaning for employees and to guide members back to core values of the organization. For example, a principal of an elementary school may tell the story of a student who emulates her teacher in order to reveal how much impact teachers have on children. An executive director of a nonprofit organization will tell a story of the organization's founder by describing the founder's personality, character, and vision to motivate current employees in their work. The choice of the stories, the characters chosen, the timing of the story, and the details emphasized will create memorable stories that stay within the minds of organizational members. Leaders can create organizational stories that will be passed on throughout the life cycle of their organizations.

Culturally intelligent leaders can shape intercultural understanding by utilizing several methods that address the underlying assumptions, beliefs, and values of its members; however, this is not an easy task. As indicated, culture oftentimes consists of unconscious behaviors, values, and assumptions that develop over time and changes may occur as new associates enter into the organization. Too often, leaders will neglect to solicit information from their employees in building the organization's culture and values. This fallacy, often unintentional, can harm the organization and affect its leadership.

The following exercise will help you to identify stories that support intercultural interactions and understanding of culture in your place of work. By reflecting on these exercises, you will learn what stories drive your organization and what ones might be discarded:

1. In the space below, list the types of jokes about intercultural work that are told in your organization. If you know the words to the jokes, write them down.

2. Write down all the common phrases that are spoken in your organization related to intercultural understanding such as, "Here's *another* meeting we're required to attend on diversity," or "I'll work with this person but only because I have to."

3. Think of one common story that has been told in your organization. It could be a story of why your organization thinks diversity and culture is important to the work or why certain people leave the organization.

As you take a look at your responses, think about the following questions:

- What are the common stories in your organization?
- Are the stories generally positive or negative?
- What is your role in creating these stories?
- As a leader, what stories, if any, can you change in your organization?
- What steps, if any, will you take to change your organizational stories?

Chapter Summary

- Changing behaviors requires cultural strategic thinking and mindfulness in order to recognize which behaviors are inappropriate and which are desirable.
- Self-concept is critical to one's adaptation. Self-concepts are developed over time, they are dynamic, and they are organized.
- Cognitive dissonance can interrupt one's self-concept. Dissonance between one's self-concept and what is heard or observed causes one to feel uncomfortable, anxious, fearful, and in the learning process, makes a person less likely to learn the new information.
- Adaptation of one's behaviors requires management of the internal change process and one's responses to it. Knowledge of your behaviors during change or transitions can help you to identify the emotions and thoughts you have that are counterproductive to your ability to adapt.

- Linguistic relativity is the idea that language shapes world views and also shapes behaviors. Words, and the understanding of words, take on many forms in different cultures; words may be understood differently in different cultures.
- Cultures communicate in different ways, and as a result, the behaviors of people are different. It is important that, as a leader, while paying attention to the behaviors, you recognize the intention of the communication versus the impact.
- To change one's behaviors, you must learn to change your mind. This requires the ability to think in a culturally strategic manner and to be mindful of your thoughts and behaviors. Once you identify the situation, the thoughts you have about the situation, and the emotions you feel in the situation, you have a greater chance of changing the behavior.
- Storytelling is a strategy to use when changing behaviors. Stories can unite people of different cultures in recognizing core organizational values.

CHAPTER 7

Cultural Intelligence in Action

In the previous chapters, you have been presented with the three principles of cultural intelligence (CI): cultural strategic thinking, motivation, and behavior. This chapter provides case studies[1] of leaders and managers who must find solutions to working through intercultural problems and situations. Each case study is followed by an activity to help you apply your understanding of the cultural intelligence principles; then, it is followed by a list that outlines sample ideas related to the questions in the activity. The following are your instructions:

- Read the case studies.
- Answer the questions in the activity section.
- Review ideas.

Case Study 1: Resistance to Change

Victor is the head of a division in a state agency. He has been in his management position for 15 years and has worked his way up to his current position. Throughout his career, he has seen many people leave and join the department. He has stayed because he enjoys public service and working with familiar faces in the agency. He also knows that he brings his many years of experiences in a public agency to the table when solving problems. His personality fits the working environment of a state agency; he likes working with the familiarity of rules and procedures.

Victor is proud of his service, but he is really looking forward to his retirement, which, for him, is not coming soon enough. Within the last few years, lots of changes have occurred on a department level that is also changing many of the familiar procedures, rules, and norms that Victor has been accustomed to during his 25 years in the department. Some of these changes include hiring younger staff, reorganization of job responsibilities, performance plans to increase staff competencies and skills in new areas, and recent layoffs to help balance the budget.

As part of his attempt to make his mark on the division, and to bring in past experiences that he thinks can be of value, Victor proposed numerous ideas for the division at a staff meeting. His staff—*which, in recent years, has become increasingly more diverse in demographics and cultural backgrounds*—suggests improvements and changes to his ideas. They are not so sure that his changes are the most appropriate given the overall strategic directions of the department. Furthermore, they are not sure how they can implement strategies when the ideas call for outdated resources and technology. Some of the younger staff members are more vocal and mention recent trends and practices in strategic thinking that could be more beneficial to accomplishing the division goals.

Victor views these suggestions as attacks directed at him and as resistance on the part of the staff. He feels like every time he makes a suggestion, he is thrown a curveball from one of the younger staff members. Why is this happening to him now? He knows he has to manage this. He cannot let this type of dynamic go on for an additional 5 years—or could he?

1. What cultural assumptions fuel Victor's perspective as a leader of a state agency?
2. Where does Victor's motivation to lead come from?
3. How would you describe Victor's self-concept and the influence of it on his leadership?

Reflection

Victor has several cultural assumptions that can be broken down into different cultural levels: individual, team, organizational, and national cultures. His assumptions and beliefs may include any of the following: working hard will get you to the top, everyone must obey rules and procedures, and you must have experience in order to know what you are doing in a job. This could be why he feels attacked when his younger employees make suggestions. It is also important to note that Victor may have been raised in a homogenous culture that did not allow him to interact with others who did not share his same cultural values and belief. Victor can benefit from learning about his self-concept and how his values contribute to his management. By doing so, Victor helps his team to understand him more.

CI Model in Action

- Acquire: Victor has a lot of knowledge about working in public sector organizations. His tenure in a state agency makes him very familiar with this type of culture. But he lacks knowledge about what is unfamiliar to him, particularly around generational issues. He knows what areas of his work frustrate him; now he needs to acquire information to help him understand why they frustrate him. To improve his cultural intelligence, Victor would need to develop a plan that helps him to become more familiar with the different cultures in his work team.

- Build: To build his knowledge in cultures, Victor can develop strategies that help him connect his current cultural knowledge to the new knowledge he wants to gain. For example, he identifies that the characteristics of a younger generation are new to him. He can put together a plan where he monitors his communication with the staff to gauge whether he is really understanding what is going on. It is important here that when he builds new knowledge, he is aware of the skills he has and what he lacks when working with a younger generation.

- Contemplate: Victor's self-efficacy is an issue in this cultural situation. He has a few years left before retirement and considers giving up. He needs to make a shift, changing his attitude from one of frustration to a positive perspective. He can do this by visualizing the positive end results and reminding himself that he can and should keep trying. He needs to put in place a plan where he can monitor his internal motivation toward the issue.

- Do: It seems in this situation that change will be difficult for Victor because he is set in his ways. Victor can be mentored and coached to think about change and its impact on his situation by asking himself: What is changing, What will be different because of the change, and What will he lose? Using these three questions he will learn to identify the change and behaviors that need to change, the potential results of the change, and what beliefs and values he will need to discard in the process. By identifying specific areas of change, Victor can transition better.

Case Study 2: Young, Confident, and Moving Too Fast

Julia, who is 26 years old, recently graduated from the University of Chicago with her master's degree in social work. She is a confident young woman who is used to making quick decisions, and she greatly values her independence. She graduated at the top of her class and, throughout her course of study, was known by her peers and professors as a "go-to person" for resolving conflicts and finding strategic, innovative approaches to social work. She is highly motivated and passionate about social justice and social change issues, particularly those involving poverty and housing.

She has high expectations in her career as a social worker and has found a job working with a local nonprofit organization that provides transitional housing to people who are homeless. Her boss, Joanne, holds her in high regard, but now, in her second month of the job, Julia is increasingly annoyed by her boss's constant micromanagement and questioning of her decisions. "Come to me before you make a major decision. I don't want you to move so fast on your own," Joanne says.

Julia asks, "Have I made any mistakes so far?" "No," Joanne retorts, "but I feel that you need to check in with me before you move on with some projects. You've only been here for 2 months and there's a lot of stuff you still need to learn."

"Well, tell me what they are. I'm eager to learn everything so I can do my job better," Julia replies.

"I don't think you're ready yet. There's a lot to learn about this job. Believe me, I was like you, too, when I was younger, but over the years I've learned that it takes time and patience to do this work. It's fast paced and working in this field can be emotionally draining. We just can't afford to make mistakes when we do this work."

Julia cannot believe what she is hearing. Here she is, eager and motivated to take on more work, and Joanne says that it is too overwhelming. She thinks, *"What kind of work environment is this that won't let me use skills and knowledge?"*

This week, Julia is furious. She worked on a slide presentation for a major donor and prepared a report about the progress of the organization's clients, for which Joanne commended her. Nevertheless, she was told bluntly that she could not be a part of the donor meeting. "This is ridiculous," Julia thinks. "I'm moving on. I'll stay here until I get something better, but I sure am going to start looking around."

1. What beliefs and values "root" Joanne and Julia to their self-concepts?
2. What suggestions do you have for Joanne and Julia when working with a person of another generation?
3. How would you suggest Joanne and Julia use the cultural intelligence principles to resolve this intercultural situation?

Reflection

Julia believes she is a fast learner, and she has a high level of confidence. She wants to quickly move up the ladder but feels that Joanne, her manager, is creating barriers. Joanne does not feel this way and believes that she knows best, given her experiences in the industry. Both Joanne and Julia have beliefs about who they are and what they are capable of doing. Additionally, they both are making assumptions about each other, which leads to their behaviors. It would be helpful to both individuals to conduct an exercise that explores their behaviors, the thoughts that accompany the behaviors, and the emotions they feel.

CI Model in Action

- Acquire: Joanne is in a formal position of leadership in this case study. As a leader who wants to be culturally intelligent, Joanne would seek to understand what experiences she has had in the past that contribute to her thinking about individuals like Julia. She needs to make the connection between this information and the new information about what she wants to experience related to generational culture. It would be helpful for Joanne to think about how she feels and what she might suspect Julia to feel in their interactions. Identifying emotions and feelings can serve as a great source of feedback to help Joanne comprehend the full picture of the situation.

- Build: To improve her cultural intelligence, Joanne can seek out a mentor who has worked with individuals like Julia. In CI work, it is important to be able to talk through cultural situations, particularly your plans and goals related to working with different cultural groups. In this situation, a mentor can help Joanne to identify the pieces of culture that she may not be picking up such as Julia's high expectations of herself, her ability to get things done in an informal work setting, and her working style preference.

- Contemplate: Joanne, in this case study, thinks that Julia is very capable to carry out projects and tasks. However, she can do more to help build her own self-efficacy as well as Julia's, thus improving both of their cultural intelligences. It is more effective if Joanne schedules weekly evaluation and progress sessions with Julia. In this session, Joanne can help Julia to understand specific outcomes and expectations as well as take the opportunity to mentor her. Developing her cultural intelligence would mean that Joanne comes to these meetings prepared to provide the right type of feedback and recognize when to provide this feedback.

- Do: Joanne is able to quickly point out what Julia's blind spots are in their interactions. But does Joanne see her own blind spots? In this component of CI, Joanne can and should evaluate her own behavior, including what she may not see because she is too focused on whether Julia will make a mistake. Her ability to adapt rests on her acknowledgement of what makes her uncomfortable when Julia performs well. Does she hold a belief or attitude about how work can be completed? Or who can do the work?

Case Study 3: Building a
Multicultural Team—Is It Worth It?

Kalia works in a large business, managing a diverse team of eight individuals. Two of her employees are in their early 20s, two in their 30s,
three in their late 40s, and one in her late 50s. Four members of her team
are Caucasian and the other four are Hispanic, African American, Asian,
and African. Her younger employees are fairly new, having been there
for less than 2 years. Most of her team members have worked with the
organization for 5 to 10 years, and her most senior staff has been there for
25 years, 10 years longer than Kalia has been in her leadership position.

Generally, team members are cordial to one another on the surface,
but Kalia knows that there are tensions among some of the staff that
have an impact on the success and productiveness of the team. She is
aware that one of the younger employees, Robert, is frequently frustrated
that his Hispanic coworker, Ana, defers authority and decision making
to others on the team. In conversations with him, she discovers that the
younger employee feels Ana should express her opinions more often.
Robert's frustration results from his beliefs that everyone on the team
should be able to contribute in a shared, democratic process. He feels that
when Ana defers her decision making to others, she is not being accountable as a team member.

Margaret, a senior member of the team, has picked up on Robert's
comments and feels that he is disrespectful of Ana's working style. She has
mentioned to him that it could be a "cultural thing" and that he should
learn to adapt his behavior and working style to better meet her needs.
In response, Robert mutters, "Whatever. You don't know anything about
us." Responses like this have led Margaret to believe that he is disrespectful of her knowledge and tenure in the organization.

Frankly, Kalia is tired of managing people's personalities. She feels
that people should just learn to adapt to each other's working styles. Even
though she believes this, she also believes that a good leader has to unite
the team, no matter their differences and working styles. This year, she
has made it a goal of hers, and of the team, to resolve these intercultural
issues. But given her previous attempts, she does not have high hopes
for a successful outcome. The last time she tried to resolve intercultural
team issues, she felt like a complete failure. She is concerned about the

employees' responses to this next attempt. In fact, every time she thinks about that meeting, she flinches. She just did not have the skill sets to facilitate the conversation in their last meeting. She wonders if this next try will progress her team in any way or whether it will just be another failure.

1. How do you describe Kalia's self-efficacy?
2. How does Kalia's self-efficacy impact her leadership?
3. What strategies do you recommend to Kalia to help her improve her cultural intelligence?
4. What suggestions do you have for Kalia in leading her staff to be a culturally intelligent team?

Reflection

Kalia works with a multicultural team, and each member has his or her own individual differences. In a situation like this, it would be helpful for Kalia to explore her motivation and self-efficacy for managing multicultural teams and resolving intercultural conflicts. Her self-efficacy can, and does, have an impact on her leadership. If her employees see that she is not confident or able to resolve conflicts, they may disregard the positional power she has as a leader. Because it seems as if she is overwhelmed, it would be helpful to her to break down her goal of creating a culturally intelligent team into manageable, small goals. She can also help others to recognize the basics of cultural differences in the workplace and the positive ways in which differences can be used to ignite their work.

CI Model in Action

- Acquire: As a leader, it is important for Kalia to understand the types of individual and team culture that are present in her work place. Her frustration about her team is a result of not knowing what to do based on her limited perspective of culture. Broadening her viewpoint to understand the value dimensions of culture such as language, power, authority, and gender can help her to make more sense of the situation. As Kalia learns this new information, she can evaluate her progress by identifying points in her interactions where the value dimensions appear and whether she has accurately assessed the situation. Understanding the particulars about culture will help her to grasp the cultural dynamics at play.

- Build: Resolving cultural conflicts can be overwhelming, especially to someone, like Kalia, who wants to avoid it. In this situation, Kalia will need to help resolve the conflict among team members. She can do this in two ways: first, by helping team members to understand their individual working styles, and in this case, taking the members that have the most conflict aside for discussions. Second, she can help them understand how individual cultures contribute to a team culture by describing the type of team she wants to build. She can mediate the conflict by herself or bring in an outside mediator.

- Contemplate: Kalia's anxiety and self-induced stress is a barrier to her success as a leader. She believes she does not have the skill sets to facilitate future meetings, and her thoughts are focused on this point. She cannot shy away from the situation, thus it would be helpful to Kalia to create smaller action steps for her team and herself to meet the larger goal. She would need to stay calm and focused on the task.

- Do: Kalia's internal motivation will be a huge assistance to her managing the situation. She knows she does not have the skill sets to facilitate the next meeting, but she can find ways to build her skills, or she can bring in an outside person to help her mediate. If she chooses to facilitate the meeting on her own, she will need to reflect and identify the skill sets she would need. She can do this by first identifying the thoughts she has related to the situation and the behaviors that accompany the thoughts. In doing this, she may find out that she has the skills to facilitate but needs more confidence.

Case Study 4: A New Leadership Culture

It's been 6 months since Kolab was hired to lead a large, nonprofit organization called, International Education Center (IEC), which provides international education and information to the citizens of a midwestern state. The organization provides opportunities for individuals to learn about different cultures and to gain an understanding about their role as citizens of the world. It does this by connecting the people of the state with visitors from all over the world in order to meet with and learn from one another.

Prior to the job at the IEC, Kolab directed national programming and services for the Office of Refugee Resettlement (ORR) in Washington, DC. Before her job at the ORR, she worked for an international relief agency and traveled extensively throughout Southeast Asia and Africa, working in the organization's field offices, managing its daily operations.

Kolab, born in Cambodia, fled with her parents to the United States as a refugee during the regime of Pol Pot and the Khmer Rouge (the followers of the Communist Party who ruled Cambodia from 1975 to 1979). Her experiences growing up as a refugee fuel her motivation and passion for international work. It also shaped her expectations and working style. She is known to her colleagues as a "go-getter" and a "high performer."

The board of trustees thought Kolab's international experiences and goal-oriented, achievement-focused attitude was just what they needed to expand the organization on a national level. The previous president, Hanh, did not have the strategic thinking and vision to move IEC, even though she was very effective at building relationships throughout the state. After 10 years with IEC, Hanh decided to step down from her leadership role. This gave the board of directors an opportunity to hire someone like Kolab who can challenge employees and push the organization to reach its financial and fundraising goals.

Since Kolab's hire, employee productivity and motivation has decreased. Staff used to enjoy coming to work, talking with one another, and planning programs and services for the community. Now they come to work because "we need a paycheck," and they accomplish their tasks because "Kolab told me to do so." There is no enthusiasm for the mission of the organization and the vision for the new work that Kolab and the directors created in a strategic planning meeting. A couple of times, when Kolab passed employee cubicles, she heard comments like, "She works us all like we don't have a personal life," "She's so impersonable," "I miss just chatting with people," and "Hanh was never like this. She always made time to talk to us."

Just last week, Kolab had a staff meeting, and the majority of staff sauntered in late. Throughout the meeting, they gave her blank stares, and, as soon as the meeting was over, they quickly left. Kolab is tired of the staff attitudes and behaviors. "The culture of this organization can't operate the way it used to. I am determined to change it," she thinks to herself.

1. How does Kolab's self-concept influence her ability to lead?
2. What cultural value dimensions does the organization operate under? What about Kolab?
3. What cultural intelligence strategies do you recommend for Kolab and her employees?

Reflection

There are several issues here that Kolab needs to work through. First, Kolab has a specific leadership style that she likes to use. Her style is task- and goal-oriented and is influenced by her upbringing. Her beliefs and her attitude are exactly what the board wants, but it is drastically different than the leadership style and organizational culture that is familiar to the employees. Second, Kolab wants the culture of the organization to move toward accountability, goals, and achievement; this is not to say that the organization was not goal-oriented before. Kolab's vision for the organization's goals, and how to get there, is a departure from what the cultural norm dictated in the past. Third, the staff has a self-concept that was developed as a result of Hanh's leadership influence. They are feeling a dissonance between their self-concept and the new one that Kolab wants to enforce. Kolab would need to address all these areas and find strategies that help to keep her staff motivated during this time of change.

CI Model in Action

- Acquire: There are multiple levels of culture at work in this case study, particularly how individual cultural differences are expressed and interpreted. Kolab has an approach to work that differs from her employees; most of the approach is based on her personal experiences and history as a refugee.

As a leader practicing cultural intelligence, Kolab will need to take a look at her self-concept and how it differs or corresponds with her staff. She can do this in two ways: first, by exploring her own personal history and second, by getting to know her staff as individuals. The knowledge she gains about herself and others will bridge her understanding of individual cultural differences and how they are expressed in an organization.

- Build: Kolab was hired because she is a "go-getter," which typically means that she is achievement focused and oriented. Her staff interprets this as "impersonable." To build an understanding of cultural differences, Kolab can build into her personal development plan ways to observe and listen to her staff. As an observer, she can pick up on verbal and non-verbal cues in her environment, thus helping her pay attention to her surroundings. By actively listening to her staff, she will learn how to adapt her behavior appropriately for the situation she is in.

- Contemplate: Kolab has a high ability to be resilient, which she developed as part of her personality and individual culture because of her experience as a refugee. This will be helpful to her in staying positive about the situation. However, one of the things she could improve on is her ability to gauge the emotions of her staff during their interactions. She is not accurately perceiving the thoughts and emotions, thus she is unable to handle the relationships in a way that is appropriate.

- Do: Kolab is trying to change the culture of the organization. As a leader, she needs to recognize that cultural shifts can be difficult, and it is her responsibility as a leader to help her employees make the changes successfully. She can help change cultural behavior through the use of stories. She can strategize this in different ways. She can set time for people to share the stories of the "old culture" and what they would like to see in the new culture. She can, using the power of words and language, share stories of herself, her vision, and where she would like the organization to be. She can combine her stories with the stories of her employees to create a unified story.

Case Study 5: Marketing the Right Messages

Diane is the president of a public relations and marketing company that is in its 10th year of business. The company has a wide range of clients in the government, in private businesses, and in the nonprofit sector. It provides media strategies, designs and develops media campaigns, and advises companies with their marketing plans.

Recently, she negotiated a contract with a local nonprofit organization interested in creating a media campaign to address domestic abuse and violence issues in disadvantaged communities. The nonprofit provides transitional housing, mental health services, and counseling and education to women and children seeking safety from their abusers. Residents are primarily women and children, of which 87% are African American, 10% are Hispanic, and 3% are Asians.

The nonprofit wants to reach out to the Hispanic and Asian communities. They want to provide information and education, and create awareness in the communities about their services. Felicia, the executive director, described to Diane what they have already done as an organization and the challenges they have encountered. She identifies these challenges as English language barriers, trust issues working with an organization not in their community, and different ways that the cultures respond to domestic violence and abuse issues. Felicia wants a campaign that will break these barriers and give the organization an opportunity to begin working with Hispanic and Asian communities.

Diane's company has never worked on a media campaign such as the one presented to her. Although they have done campaigns and advised on strategies in the social services field, the topic of domestic abuse and violence, especially in Hispanic and Asian communities, is new to her and her employees. She is not worried about reaching the African American community, since she is from that community and has been successful in creating a variety of strategies and campaigns.

She knows that her employees will need to do some research before creating media messages that speak to the Hispanic and Asian markets. She is up for the challenge and thinks this project will expand the company in a new and exciting direction. In addition, it will help her staff improve their knowledge and work with the diverse communities within their city.

1. How can Diane and her employees use the idea of "self-concept" to help them in their work?
2. What cultural value dimensions should Diane and her employees be aware of when working with Hispanic and Asian communities?

Reflection

Diane knows that there is culturally specific information and knowledge missing in her organization that could help the business execute a media campaign. Using cultural strategic thinking, she can outline the outcomes of what she wants to achieve by looking at the gaps. Diane's team can also use Hofstede's cultural value dimensions to gain an understanding of each cultural group. By doing this, they can learn about the nature of power, relationships, and identity that exists in each group. They may find that one cultural value dimension takes more precedence than others in a cultural group. As a result of their cultural strategic thinking, they will come to learn about themselves as an organization and as individuals. When they do this, they will be better prepared to serve the client and the community.

CI Model in Action

- Acquire: Diane and her team can acquire cultural knowledge by identifying what they currently know and what they would like to learn. For example, if they know the communities they need to reach have language challenges, the team can describe what they would like to learn to overcome those barriers. Based on this first piece, the team can develop strategies to bridge the gaps between their knowledge. As they implement the plan, they can monitor and evaluate the success of the strategies.
- Build: It may be helpful to Diane and her team to create an advisory group of people from the communities they would like to reach. A group like this can provide them with peer learning opportunities and offer guidance in the project. Additionally, they can build their cultural intelligence by attending local events or talking to people from the communities they will market to. This provides them with an

opportunity to check their assumptions and gather cultural information and facts.

- Contemplate: Diane seems ready to address the challenges, thus indicating that she is motivated and confident that herself and her team will end up successful. To keep their spirits high, the team can identify moments of success from past projects as well as identify current successes. Creating environments where her team feels successful in their job and accomplishment of goals will help Diane and her team to stay positive and focused. Doing this helps to increase their levels of self-efficacy and mindfulness.

- Do: As the team performs their strategies, their focus must be on cultivating respectful relationships with the communities. Diane and her team will need to pay attention to how relationships are developed as well as how relationships are interpreted within the communities. Understanding this helps them shape messages that are not offensive or shaming.

Case Study 6: On Opposite Political Sides

"Did you see last night's primary?" Scott says to his staff during their morning coffee break as a team.

"Yeah. McAllister is going down! That 'lefty' annoys me. Talking about big government and ways to spend our hard earned money. No one in their right mind will vote for him. I'll be celebrating when he loses come November," Joe notes.

Scott replies, "If this liberal trend keeps up we won't have any more freedoms. None of us will have jobs when big government steps in." He sees his colleagues nodding their heads enthusiastically and hears echoes from his team, "Yep, that's right."

Scott notices that Amber, who he hired as a sales assistant to the team, is quiet. Maybe she is one of them, he thinks. "Hey Amber, you're kind of looking quiet over there. What are you, red or blue?"

Amber is a bit hesitant. This is her first professional experience since graduating from college 6 months ago. Most of her teammates are in their mid-40s and have been working with the company for 10 years or more. She does not want any ill feelings, but she also does not agree with the language that is used and the conversation. She certainly does not want to create a bad image of her to her boss. "Well, I don't think it's about big taxes. I just don't like the views of the new GOP candidate," she says, carefully.

Scott quickly replies, "That doesn't matter. If you're voting liberal you're going to bankrupt our country, and that's it."

Amber is taken back by the fierceness in her boss's tone of voice and decides she will not participate in conversations like this anymore. However, in the next couple of months, her team finds ways to comment about her political views. They have even nicknamed her, calling her "*Lefty.*" She finds it disturbing that every time she speaks up about her viewpoints, her team instantly fires back with a counterargument—Scott included. When she has gently brought up the issue to her team, they laugh and say, "We're just joking. Don't be so sensitive, Lefty."

Over time, Amber's motivation and passion for her work decreases. She has become more guarded in her comments, and, at times, she argues back with just as much passion as the others. On the surface, the team gets along but the tensions impact their work together. Amber notices it but is afraid to say anything to Scott. She decides she wants to find another job—it is just easier that way.

1. What values and beliefs shape the behaviors of the sales team?
2. How is Scott's leadership behavior impacting the team?
3. As Scott's supervisor, what suggestions or course of actions would you take with Scott?

As a leader, Scott needs to evaluate his self-concept and the impact it has on the team's culture. Having awareness for how he learned his belief systems and the ways in which the beliefs and attitudes influence the team environment can help Scott to build a more inclusive team. As a leader, he needs to build all areas of his cultural intelligence (CI) including helping his team to understand their ability to work with different cultural situations. If they do not, they isolate anyone who is a part of their team that does not hold the same political beliefs.

CI Model in Action

- Acquire: First, Scott must determine the gaps in knowledge
  that he and his team members have related to different political
  beliefs. Many of his team members operate from one particular
  belief system, which they now consider a team characteristic
  and norm. Using cultural strategic thinking, he could assess the
  team's understanding of culture, assess the gaps in knowledge,
  and create a vision or goal for what they would like to achieve
  around cultural understanding.

- Build: A useful exercise for the team would be to help them
  change the types of questions they ask each other. Making
  the shift from judgment to learning can provide them with a
  different perspective. For example, rather than ask a judgment
  question like "Are you with us or not?" Scott and his team can
  ask learning questions such as, "Help me to understand why
  you agree with the other candidate."

- Contemplate: Using mindfulness techniques, the team can
  evaluate how the political conversations and belief systems
  "box them" into a specific way of thinking about their worlds.
  This would require that they are active listeners and observ-
  ers of the conversation, suspending their judgments of other
  beliefs and norms. It would serve them well to also learn how
  to manage their emotions and be able to adapt their behaviors
  by recognizing the emotions of others.

- Do: Finally, it would also be useful if Scott and his team took
  part in an exercise to identify the behaviors that are disruptive and inappropriate. Once the behaviors are called out, they
  could assess the thought patterns that support the behaviors
  and the emotions that arise because of the behaviors.

Case Study 7: From Hometown to Global Village

Community Action and Development (CAD) is an economic development center located in a small town a few miles outside of Fargo,
North Dakota. Lori has served as its president for the past 10 years. The
organization is a resource and business development center that brings

local, regional, county, and community leaders together to partner on economic growth strategies for the region. Over the years, the organization has successfully created business financing programs, small business incubation, and new jobs, and it has established career and employment services to support local and regional business retention.

Having lived in North Dakota all her life, Lori has noticed a visible cultural change in the area. With several universities and colleges in the area that attract a diverse student body, an increasingly growing population of immigrants and refugees, and a large number of Native Americans, Lori knows that CAD will need to think differently about its work and who it serves. Leaders from different cultural communities have already approached the organization about potential initiatives to help develop business programs for their groups.

Lori knows that the diversity of changes can only be of benefit to North Dakota. She has read reports by the state demographer and has researched population changes in the United States, and she feels that CAD must make strategic decisions to embrace and involve the different communities in the area. If they time it right, CAD could be seen as a leader in developing services and programs that meet the needs of immigrant and Native American populations. Not only that, the labor shortage that North Dakota has seen in recent years, due to an aging population, could be addressed if the center worked on developing a new generation of workers.

Although there are many challenges to this work, there is one significant challenge that Lori is most concerned about. Her board of directors and many leaders in the community are fearful of the demographic changes. People are most concerned about illegal immigration as well as the perceived loss of German and Scandinavian culture. Lori has brought her ideas to the board; each time, she has been told, "We have to be careful with this issue" and "We're doing just fine with our programs." The board chair has even told Lori directly, "We have to respond to our constituents' concerns and right now they don't feel this is an issue they want to tackle. Let's focus on them and their businesses." Lori argued, "But, the new immigrants are our constituents too! We can't ignore them. And we haven't done all we can to help bridge trust and understanding between ourselves and the Native American tribes here. We can't keep going in this direction when the fact is that our community is changing."

Lori has recently learned about cultural intelligence (CI) as a tool in business. She wants to introduce the idea of CI to her board and staff. She thinks it will be useful for them to understand the cultural shifts the community is undergoing and to recognize their values and beliefs. What suggestions do you have for her as she implements the CI principles in her place of work?

Reflection

Lori knows that she has to be careful when talking to her board of directors. There is already tension about cultural diversity issues and lack of awareness of the changing demographics. Many in her town feel threatened and do not pay attention to the changes. Lori has several challenges ahead of her, but there are a few things she can do to make progress toward her goal:

CI Model in Action

- Acquire: She can use her experience and research around data collection to demonstrate the different ways in which the community is changing. Using data enables her to bring concrete facts to the table. Additionally, she can evaluate the board's understanding of culture and how cultural differences are played out in the community.
- Build: Lori has the opportunity to find allies and supporters of her goal who have positional power or influence with board members. She can also find members on the board that can sway or influence others to a different perspective. These strategies can help move her closer to her goal and help the board recognize the importance of cultural changes in the community.
- Contemplate: She can help her board build their self-efficacy. Because they fear the ambiguity that change brings, she can develop systems or processes that enable her board to build their self-confidence. Additionally, if the board feels any anxiety or stress related to the cultural changes, she can help create a positive environment, gently reminding them of their successes when working with similar cultural situations.

- Do: An exercise to identify cultural changes, the results of the changes, and what can be lost or gained because of change would be helpful to this organization. Through this process, board members can specifically identify and articulate where their resistance lies. Additionally, Lori has the task of painting a different picture of change for the board members that are resistant. She will need to select her words carefully and be mindful of how she communicates and responds to board members. She can adapt her behavior and how she communicates to be less threatening to board members who fear change. Paying attention to the verbal and nonverbal cues she receives from the board can move her one step closer to her goals.

Case Study 8: No Dogs Allowed

A teenaged girl, Mary, enters the Ellendale County Public Library with a small dog and heads to the "teen books" area. She sits down at one of the tables, opens up her backpack, and takes out a textbook and piece of paper. Her dog is next to her, on the floor.

At a table next to Mary sits Ron and his mother, Alice. Ron's mother is helping him with research for school. She notices the dog, gets up, and looks for a librarian. Upon finding one, she says, "My son is allergic to dogs and that girl brought a dog to the library. He's not going to be able to study with the dog around. Can you do something about this?"

Susan, the librarian, knows that the library has a "no animal policy," except for service dogs. The policy also states that the library cannot directly question patrons if the dog is a service dog. Susan looks over at Mary and does not see any visible reasons for why the dog should be there. She heads over and tells Mary that she cannot have a dog in the library.

Mary does not understand everything the librarian says because she is hearing impaired. She needs the dog to alert her to things she cannot hear. Mary responds, but Susan does not understand Mary's speech patterns.

"I'm sorry, but you're going to have to leave," Susan says with finality.

Later that day, Craig, the director of the Ellendale County Public Library system, receives a phone call from Mary's father, Joseph, who informs him about the situation. Craig's been in his position for 3 years and with the county library for 10 years. As he listens to Joseph, he realizes that there needs to be some changes to the library's policy and training for the librarians. He is going to bring up this issue at next week's management meeting and have a conversation about strategies that will resolve these issues in the future.

To help Craig prepare for his management team meeting, use the cultural intelligence principles to help him analyze the situation that has occurred. You may use the following questions to guide your thinking:

1. What does Craig need to help him think through this situation?
2. What is the culture of the library? The culture of librarians at Ellendale?
3. What behaviors can you identify? What can Craig and his management team do differently that will change this behavior?
4. How can Craig and his team use self-efficacy concepts to improve their cultural intelligence?

Reflection

There are several items at play in this situation that Craig needs to understand when speaking with his staff.

CI Model in Action

- Acquire: Craig received information only from a patron, Joseph. He is disturbed at what he hears and jumps to his own conclusions about what needs to be done. It would be appropriate to hear from the librarians and others at the library about the situation. Moreover, Craig and his team need to evaluate their own cultural intelligence when working with people who have disabilities.
- Build: Cultural strategic thinking can help them assess what gaps exist in their knowledge and understanding of people who have disabilities. As a result of the assessment, they could identify organizational goals that would be beneficial to all staff, whether these goals are related to training, policy changes, behavioral changes, or customer service improvements.
- Contemplate: The mindfulness aspect of contemplation will be useful to Craig and his team. Mindfulness opens up

possibilities in what seems like a closed ended situation. Using mindfulness as a tool, it is apparent here that there is a need for cultural sensitivity training for the librarians. But there is also a larger issue: the policies for patrons with disabilities need to be reviewed and reconsidered. It would be helpful for the management team to discuss how long ago the policies were created, what changes in the environment the library can expect (in terms of demographic and economic changes) that might impact their policies, and what the protocol is for addressing issues that are not included in the library's policies.

- Do: For Craig's team to be more adaptable, it would be helpful for them to understand their self-concepts, including the organization's self-concept. How has the organization come to understand who they are based on their expectations and responses to their patrons? How have policies been developed as a result of these responses? Where does our organizational self-concept restrict us and create barriers to a successful change? Asking these learning questions can help them shift their thinking to a different perspective.

Case Study 9: Faith and Health

Abdul Hadi is one of the 3 million Muslims living in Germany today. He has had surgery and is recovering from his operations in a hospital near his home. Anna is his nurse and is increasingly frustrated with his behavior and having to accommodate his needs. His behaviors and needs are as follows:

- Because of the nature of Abdul Hadi's surgery, it is difficult for him to take a shower or bathe himself. When preparing for prayer, he needs to cleanse himself. He needs assistance and Anna is there to provide help, but he refuses to have her help. Finding a male nurse to help bathe Abdul Hadi has been a challenge, as all of the male nurses work different shifts and are already assigned to other patients.
- As a devout Muslim, Abdul Hadi does not eat pork. Medication provided to him must not have any pork products or

alcoholic substances; he is only allowed specific medications and treatments containing these products as dictated by Islamic law.

- Abdul Hadi also has special dietary needs. Because much of the cafeteria food contains pork products, gelatin, or lard, in one form or another, it is hard to find food that fits his needs while ensuring he stays healthy and strong.
- Abdul Hadi has many relatives that visit him; as a result, the patients that share his room complain about the noise and level of activity.
- As a Muslim, he prays and needs the space to do this. He needs to have a nurse help him get out of bed. Sometimes he has called Anna to help him, but because she is attending other patients, she does not come in time to assist him.

You are Anna's supervisor. You want her to be able to work with Abdul Hadi and to provide him with the best care.

1. Using what you know about cultural intelligence, analyze the situation.
2. For each of the five behaviors and needs outlined above, find a strategy, or strategies, to resolve the issues.
3. Determine what your hospital needs to do to ensure patients are addressed with care and compassion.

CI Model in Action

- Acquire: It is important for the supervisors, including the hospital administrators, to recognize the cultural differences that exist between themselves and people of the Islamic faith. There is a specific belief and value system operating within this hospital. This system dictates how to interact with and treat patients, and as a result, policies are developed to treat and work with patients in a specific way. These ideas come into conflict when there are individuals who do not perceive care in the same way. A useful exercise for the supervisor and hospital administrators would be to identify what they currently know about the Islamic culture and what they would like to learn more about. This can include identification of organizational cultural belief systems and values related to working with patients. When they do this, it helps them to create concrete strategies for improvement.

- Build: For Anna, the supervisor can help her to assess her self-efficacy and confidence level in working with patients of different cultural and religious backgrounds. She can work with Anna to help her become a more active listener, so as to build a more trusting and respectful relationship with patients. The supervisor can also help Anna by coaching or mentoring her, which entails asking her questions, making suggestions, and exploring alternative care techniques. Doing this provides Anna and the supervisor with the opportunity to break down what is happening in the situation.

- Contemplate: It would be important for Anna to keep an open mind and suspend judgments about patient's beliefs and religious practices. She can learn to be a better observer and listener, thus allowing her to pick up cultural nuances that she may not have otherwise noticed. Her ability to manage her emotions, gauge the patient's emotions, and adapt as needed is really important in the care of patients. Because illnesses can be a large source of physical and emotional stress, Anna's assistance in helping patients to manage their emotional responses could only benefit her.

- Do: The supervisor can help Anna to learn to identify behaviors that are inappropriate and are a setback to the patient's health and well-being. Learning to name the emotions and identify the thought patterns that occur while working with Abdul Hadi can help Anna to release negative emotions and feelings she has toward the patient.

Case Study 10: An Old Boy's Club

Pattie works as a corporate lawyer at Hannigan, Fisher, and Schultz, a firm known for its work in intellectual property and securities law. Prior to her job, she served as a corporate attorney for a large Fortune 500 company located in San Jose, California. She is the mother of two young boys, 7 and 4 years old. Her husband works a full-time job as a financial manager for a prestigious financial services company. Even though Pattie and her husband lead busy professional lives, they always make sure that their two children come first. Jack, the younger of the two, was diagnosed with severe epilepsy 2 years ago, and the family wants to ensure that Jack receives the best care and attention.

In the past 7 years that Pattie has been with the firm, she has done everything she can to be promoted to partner. She has developed a large network of professional relationships. She has worked hard to demonstrate her leadership and management potential to her supervisors and has led multi-million-dollar team projects. She has brought in new business and meets all her billable hours. She does all this while attending to her family's special needs.

This year, only two associates were promoted to partner; both were men, both with the firm for less than 5 years. When she learned of this, she spoke with Robert, a senior partner and close colleague of hers: "Robert, what's going on here? I've been here for 6 years, done everything according to the book, and yet I get passed up? I thought you said you were going to go to bat for me this year?"

"I did." Robert hesitates and says, "You know, it's hard to convince a bunch of old guys that you're committed to your job."

"Commitment? What are you talking about? You, of all people, know how hard I work," Pattie replies. "Wait a minute. Is this about me working from home to take care of Jack this year?"

"Listen, it's a tough world out here. They just want to know you're going to be there for them; you know, keep bringing in the money. That's how it is around here. It's a 'do as we say or there's the door' attitude around here. I'm sorry Pattie, but I'll do what I can to support you—just hang in there."

Using your knowledge about cultural intelligence principles, analyze what you believe is happening in this firm, and then identify three suggestions you have for the leadership of this organization.

Reflection

Pattie works in a male-dominated law firm that seems to be entrenched in beliefs and values about women's work and the work of attorneys. Although she has an ally in Robert, she still feels alone and discriminated against. In a situation such as this, Robert and Pattie would need to bring to the attention of their managers the subtle and insidious ways in which gender inequality occurs in the firm. This is a huge challenge, especially when partners in the firm do not see the problem, or they view the problem as something different than gender equality.

Here is a situation in which Pattie must evaluate her beliefs and values and whether they align with the culture of the law firm. She needs to determine whether it is worth it for her to stay at the law firm or to bring more attention to the issue. Since she has Robert as an ally, and since he is a senior partner in the firm, he can be the support and advocate she needs to bring attention to the issue. Additionally, because of his position, he has the power to bring awareness of gender inequality issues to his managers and colleagues.

CI Model in Action

- Acquire: In a situation like this, organizational leaders need to shift the way they think about women's work as attorneys. There are specific beliefs and values involved, unexpressed but felt by Pattie and most likely other women in the firm. The firm of Hannigan, Fisher, and Schultz must recognize the cultural norms that sustain the behaviors. Because Robert is Pattie's ally and a senior partner, he can advocate for her, but he needs to know what cultural dynamics are occurring in the organization to be able to articulate and communicate the issues to his supervisors. As he makes his case, he can ask himself questions like "What's the big picture?" or "What's possible here?"
- Build: Robert can continue to support Pattie by acting as a coach or mentor. But, in his role as coach or mentor, he must pay attention to the cultural elements such as her gender, age, legal experience, and seniority in the firm, even

the organization's culture. These cultural elements will likely impact the types of suggestions he has for her and the kind of support he can give her.

- Contemplate: In this situation, because the organization is entrenched in very specific belief and value systems, Pattie may never get to be a partner. She will need to consider what keeps her motivated to be in the job and why she would want to work for the firm. She cannot allow the situation to lower her self-efficacy; rather, she must make the most of it given her situation. As she learns more about her values and goals (self-concept), she may find that she no longer wants to work in the firm.

- Do: Because Pattie cannot change the minds of her employers, the best she can do is to understand who she is in the situation and how she wants to manage it. She can make the situation worse by holding a negative attitude or she can choose to manage her emotions effectively until she decides what to do. Opening herself to other possibilities might seem challenging given her family situation; but as she adapts to the changes in her life, she will eventually transition into a better place.

CHAPTER 8

The Future of
Cultural Intelligence

One day an elephant saw a hummingbird lying flat on its back on the ground; its feet in the air.

"What are you doing," asked the elephant.

The hummingbird replied, "I heard that the sky might fall today. If that happens, I am ready to do my part to hold it up."

The elephant laughed and mocked the bird. "You think those feet can hold up the sky?"

"Not alone," said the bird. "But we must each do what we can, and this is what I can do."

—Adapted from R. MacDonald, *Three minute tales*

How can we ensure that our leadership matters at a very deep level? What can we do to cultivate awareness for cultural intelligence in all individuals within our organizations? As this Chinese fable tells, we have a responsibility to one another.

This book began with the idea that there are important factors changing the way we do our work, the way we connect with one another, and how we perceive one another. Technological, political, and environmental changes are fueling a global economy that is quickly flattening; our interdependence with one another goes beyond our relationships in the workplace. All of these factors create new world experiences.

When asked to describe the "person of tomorrow," Carl Rogers,[1] one of the founders of the field of humanistic psychology, said that in the new world, people will have a desire for creating wholeness in life, thought, and feelings. This "person of tomorrow" will have a need to find and create new experiences that bring a deeper understanding of humanity to work. Similarly, Frances Hasselbein, the former CEO of Girl Scouts, said that people in our societies are looking to find themselves. There is a thirst for personal and inner knowledge and a thirst to understand how this information will uncover a more profound awareness for how we relate to one another.

There are four areas in which cultural intelligence will significantly improve our understanding of culture and intercultural work. These areas are reframing, adaptive work, systems thinking, and consciousness.

Reframing

Leaders must be able to reframe their thinking and practice of culture. Cultural intelligence is a tool that helps move leaders from a place of single perspective to one that has multiple filters for sorting through and navigating the cultural intelligence labyrinth. The idea and the practice of shifting your perspective (reframing)[2] allows leaders to move from mindlessness to mindfulness. It enables leaders to identify old thought patterns that lead to destructive and negative behaviors, which, in turn, impact and influence one's leadership.

One of the areas that cultural intelligence can help us reframe is the changing demographics and environmental landscape we experience as a society. As we see globalization's effects in the world, we must reframe how to think about and include different stakeholders in our work. Who we involve matters. Who we ask to be part of the conversation matters. And, most importantly, how we engage them is critical. Cultural intelligence, when used, can help to move people from the margins of work to the center, thus engaging them and creating systems of inclusion rather than representation.

I found reframing to be beneficial to leaders when developing long-lasting and meaningful intercultural relationships. For this to happen, it is vital for leaders and organizations to change their thinking about and practices concerning relationships. Leaders can create a shift in cultivating authentic relationships with different cultural groups or individuals when the questions asked are shifted from "how can this relationship help me to reach my organizational (personal) goals" to "what can I (we) learn from this relationship, and how can the learning move us toward our vision?"

I suggested this question to a woman who manages volunteers in a nonprofit. In our brief conversation, she realized that asking the question in this way helped her to see culture and diversity as a process rather than an outcome. She realized that it was important to build relationships for diversity work, but in doing so the relationships built can have a larger impact than the diversity efforts themselves. By asking questions such as "what forms of relationships need to exist in this organization," "what do relationships mean to this organization," and "how do people in this organization work together" enables the organization to become a learning organization based around diversity and culture.

Asking these questions enables people to be more authentic and to understand how relationships are created. This is a critical element in cultural intelligence work as it helps leaders to tap into the power that relationships have in building trust and unity. When we engage in this type of work, we reframe how we think about culture as it relates to power, decision making, authority, and leadership. We reframe who our values speak to and who they exclude, and we gain clarity about where our responsibility within our societies exists.

Adaptive Work

It is clear that the practice of cultural intelligence forces leaders to be more adaptive to their surroundings. Adaptive work requires a change in values, beliefs, or behavior.[3] Furthermore, it requires leaders to lead through conflicting values held by different groups and to eliminate the gap between the values people have and the realities of their lives. Ronald Heifetz wrote, "Adapting to human challenges requires that we go beyond the requirements of simply surviving. We perceive problems whenever circumstances do not conform to the way we think things ought to be. Thus, adaptive work involves not only the assessment of reality but also the clarification of values."[4]

Leaders are defined by their values, their beliefs, and their character. To be culturally intelligent means that you must constantly review, revise, and reflect upon your personal value systems and how these systems impact your cultural interactions. Leaders must understand and articulate what values drive their behaviors and attitudes. This means that leaders must question and challenge, that they explore the deeper stories that give life to their belief systems, and that they are courageous enough to give themselves a "reality check" for any dissonance surfacing between their beliefs and actions.

Too often, I see organizations develop assessments and tools to measure the effectiveness of "the organization as a system," and forget about the most important system, the "personal value system" that drives most of organizational processes and thinking. By doing this, organizational leaders expect the organization to adapt but do not have the support of its workers. We need to be reminded that organizational systems come about because there are people within the organization who are driven by their personal values and beliefs. Organizations can adapt if the people within them are given the opportunity and resources to adapt.

Interdependency

Martin Luther King, Jr., said that "Whatever affects one directly, affects all indirectly." Relationships and interdependence are at the core of our survival. Peter Senge wrote that leaders of the future must have the skill set to "see patterns of interdependency."[5] We live in an interdependent world; our actions and choices know no boundaries. Senge suggests that we must see the connections and relationships between, among, and within systems—cultural, political, legal, social, economic, familial, and so on. We need to be able to live effectively with one another, and if we can "see systemic patterns and understand the forces driving a system," we can "start to see where the system is headed if nothing changes."[6]

To begin to see interdependence, culturally intelligent leaders need to be clear about their purpose in working with cultural groups, people, and processes. Purpose, in culturally intelligent leadership, is to understand oneself in relationship to what is being sought. In other words, understanding and exploring your motivations, your passion, and your personal journey must serve as a foundation for reaching the desired vision to create cultural understanding and awareness. You must personally explore and identify what it would mean to the organization, and most importantly to its people, if diversity and culture of thoughts, ideas, people, and systems did not exist.

Simply asking yourself and others, "if we did not do this work, what would be lost," can help people to understand the systemic nature of culture. I once worked with a manager who asked this question of himself and then of his staff. The result was a deep and authentic dialogue about the responsibility that each person brings to the process. They understood that culture and diversity was not something to control or "manage," rather it was a human element that needed to be nurtured and cared for by everyone. The intercultural work to be explored involved everyone, no matter what level of cultural consciousness they came into the organization with. In the end, people in the organization gained an understanding for the different notions of diversity, a more clear purpose and passion for intercultural interactions, and enthusiastic support for creating a culturally inclusive environment.

Consciousness

As we progress in our understanding of culture we learn through our cognition what it takes to be a leader in an intercultural world. What is required, as evident in the idea of cultural intelligence, is a more holistic, paradoxical picture of leadership. The picture is one that must engage people's whole self, including the emotional, physical, mental, social, and spiritual domains.

This picture of leadership also forces us to recognize that the opposites we see, for example individualism and collectivism, are not in conflict; rather, they complement each other, enabling us to look at our individual and group strengths and our weaknesses in their totality. Opposites are not to demonstrate a "better than the other" dichotomy; instead, opposites create harmony, helping us to discover where we have been out of balance. Culturally intelligent leaders know they must balance the paradoxes of life: judge and learn, individual and group, strength and weakness, old and new, mindfulness and mindlessness, possible and impossible, and so on.

We are, as Carl Rogers noted, in a time where consciousness is critical to our self-development and, thus, the development of others. Through consciousness-raising activities such as cultural intelligence, we have the opportunity to let go of our limiting thoughts and behaviors. This consciousness creation is what Mary Parker Follet noted as both the social and political force of the future. It is through this creation, a collective conscious, that creative forces will emerge and work through the chaos and complexity of our times.

A Return to the Cultural Labyrinth

Joseph Campbell[7] said that by going down into the abyss, we remember the treasures of life. In cultural intelligence, leaders must be able to raise their levels of collective cultural consciousness by seeking out the challenges, or our "abyss." It is often difficult to disclose one's weaknesses, one's fears, and one's vulnerabilities concerning cultural diversity: The abyss is not really a comfortable place to be, but it does serve as an opportunity to explore one's self-concept. Cultural intelligence provides leaders with a chance to expand their capacities to become better cross-cultural leaders.

In the end, when you reach your destination, you will be changed. In our cultural intelligence journey, we all return to our core, our home, our center. We do not come back as the same person, because the world we left that was familiar to us is now unfamiliar. Campbell said that when we return to our true selves—our authentic selves—we need to be willing to rid ourselves of the life we have planned in order to enjoy the life that waits. Once you begin the work of cultural intelligence, you can no longer be the same person; you cannot go back to who you were and pick up the pieces as you left them. Your leadership story is different, and how you engage with people of different cultural backgrounds will be different.

If you truly do work that is culturally intelligent, work that is meaningful and intentional, then you will come to realize that differences in cultures promote a diversity of thinking, innovative practices, and ideas that take you out of mindlessness. Cultural intelligence keeps you alert and attentive to challenges in order to help you reach your highest potential. In business, culture's impact is to constantly test an organization's ability to be adaptable and flexible—to be the best by letting go of old assumptions and biases. It has always been the role of culture to help us let go of what we think we know and open our eyes to the responsibility we all have, as leaders, in shaping a better society.

Notes

Preface

1. Hubbard (2002), p. 1.
2. Lakoff (2006), p. 1.
3. Wheatley (n.d.), p. 4.
4. Lakoff (2006), p. 4.
5. Drucker (1994), p. 7.
6. Pink (2005).
7. Gardner (2006).
8. Csikszentmihalyi (1996).
9. House, et al. (2004), p. 15.
10. This definition of culture is adapted from Edgar Schein's definition found in "Organizational Culture and Leadership" 2010.

Introduction

1. Friedman (2007).
2. Canton (2007), p. 50.
3. Canton (2007), p. 60.
4. Canton (2007), p. 90.
5. U.S. Census (2009).
6. Lein (2004), p. 28.
7. Catalyst (2004).
8. Toossi (2006).
9. Toossi (2006).
10. Washington Times, (2010).
11. House and Javidan (2002), p. 1.

Chapter 1

1. Mitchell (1988).
2. Lawler and Worley (2006).
3. Bennis (1985).
4. Bennis (1985).

5. Taylor (1999).
6. Goldsmith (2006).
7. Salzberg (2008), p. 123.
8. Couto (1995).
9. Koopman, Hartog, and Konrad (1999).
10. Goldsmith, Greenberg, Robertson, and Hu-Chan (2003).
11. Bennis (1985), p. 3.
12. Goldsmith et al. (2003), p. 7.
13. Derr, Roussillon, and Bournois (2002), p. 298.
14. Northouse (2007), pp. 15–108.
15. Mutabazi (2002), p. 204.
16. Schein (2006), p. 259.
17. Kennedy (2008), pp. 35–40.
18. *Human resource management guide* (n.d.).
19. Lencioni (2002).
20. Kennedy (2008).
21. Bolman and Deal (2008).
22. Heifetz (1994).

Chapter 2

1. Langer (1990).
2. Katie (2002).
3. This definition of culture has been adapted from Edgar Schein's definition of culture.
4. Hofstede (1991).
5. Hofstede (1991), p. 4.
6. Senge (1990), pp. 8–9.
7. Irving (1973), pp. 19–25.
8. Meharbian (1971).
9. Campbell (1988).
10. Geertz (1973).
11. Hofstede (2001).
12. Hofstede (2001).
13. Hofstede (2001).
14. Hofstede (2001).
15. Hall (1981).
16. Cox (1994), p. 108.
17. Cox (1994), p. 106.
18. House, Hanges, Javidan, Dorfman, and Gupta (Eds.) (2004).
19. House and Javidan (2004), pp. 11–13.

Chapter 3

1. Earley and Mosakowski (2004), p. 140.
2. Earley, Ang, and Tan (2006), p. 6.
3. Thomas and Inkson (2003), p. 14.
4. Darlington (1996), p. 53.
5. Earley et al. (2006), p. 27.
6. Earley and Peterson (2004), p. 105.
7. Carlson (2005), p. 130.
8. Gardner (1983).
9. Earley and Peterson (2004), p. 101.
10. Thomas and Inkson (2003).
11. Earley and Peterson (2004), p. 105.
12. Goleman (2006), pp. 83–84.
13. Earley and Peterson (2004).
14. Carlson (2005), p. 50.
15. Campbell (1988).

Chapter 4

1. Earley and Peterson (2004), p. 104.
2. Flavell (1979).
3. Bennett (1933).
4. G. Menefee (personal communication, May 12, 2010).
5. Adams (2004).
6. Earley and Peterson (2004).

Chapter 5

1. Bandura (1974).
2. Goleman (1995).
3. Goleman (1995).
4. Frankl (1984).
5. Boyatzis and McKee (2005), p. 112.
6. Sumedho (2001).
7. Langer (1989).
8. Bandura (1994).
9. Kouzes and Posner (2002).
10. Bandura (1994).

Chapter 6

1. Earley and Peterson (2004), p. 109.

2. Thomas and Inkson (2003), p. 58.

3. Mead (1925).

4. Purkey (1988).

5. This exercise was found by The Center for Positive Organizational Scholarship at the University of Michigan, Ross School of Business, http://www.bus.umich.edu/Positive/POS-Teaching-and-Learning/ReflectedBestSelfExercise.htm

6. See the organization's website for more information: http://www.via character.org/

7. See the organization's website for more information: http://www.enneagram institute.com/

8. Palmer (1998).

9. Tavris and Aronson (2007), p. 29.

10. Lammers (June 8, 2010). The Dominion Post. *Bizarre first training hit out for All Whites*. Retrieved from http://www.stuff.co.nz/dominion-post/sport/football/3785307/Bizarre-first-training-hit-out-for-All-Whites

11. Cashman (1999), pp. 87–88.

12. Wheatley (2006), p. 82.

13. Bridges (2004).

14. Fadiman (1998).

15. Whorf (1956).

16. Earley, Ang, and Tan (2006), p. 83.

17. Hall (1990).

18. Hurtado (1996).

19. Hurtado (1996), p. 382.

20. Rogers and Steinfatt (1999), p. 151.

21. Selko (2007). *Industry Week*. "CEO Of Toy Manufacturing Company Commits Suicide". Retrieved from http://www.industryweek.com/articles/ceo _of_toy_manufacturing_company_commits_suicide_14790.aspx

22. LeBaron (2003).

23. LeBaron (2003), pp. 7–9.

24. Gardner (2004), p. 82.

Chapter 7

1. These case studies are a combination of real life stories shared by clients and colleagues I have worked with over the last 7 years as well as cases from national and international newspapers. Names of organizations and individuals have been replaced and situations have been altered to conceal their identities.

Chapter 8

1. Rogers (1980), p. 350.
2. Bolman and Deal (2008).
3. Heifetz (1994), p. 22.
4. Heifetz (1994), p. 31.
5. Senge (1990), p. 39.
6. Senge (1990), p. 39.
7. Campbell (1988).

References

Adams, M. G. (2004). *Change your questions, change your life: 7 powerful tools for life and work.* San Francisco, CA: Berrett-Koehler.

Bandura, A. (1974, December). Behavior theory and the models of man. *American Psychologist, 29*(12), 859–869.

Bandura, A. (1994). Self-efficacy. In V. S. Ramachaudran (Ed.), *Encyclopedia of Human Behavior* (Vol. 4, 71–81). New York, NY: Academic Press.

Bennett, A. (1933). *The journal of Arnold Bennett.* New York, NY: Literary Guild.

Bennis, W. (1985). *On Becoming a Leader.* New York, NY: Basic Books.

Bolman, L. G., & Deal, T. E. (2008). *Reframing organizations: Artistry, choice, and leadership* (4th ed.). San Francisco, CA: Jossey-Bass.

Bridges, W. (2004). *Transitions: Making sense of life's changes.* Cambridge, MA: De Capo Press.

Boyatzis, R. E., & McKee, A. (2005). *Resonant leadership: Renewing yourself and connecting with others through mindfulness, hope, and compassion.* Boston, MA: Harvard Business School.

Campbell, J. (1988). *The power of myth with Bill Moyers* (B. S. Flowers, Ed.). New York, NY: Bantam Doubleday.

Canton, J. (2006). *The extreme future: The top trends that will reshape the world in the next 20 years.* New York, NY: Penguin Group.

Carlson, R. (2005). *Easier than you think: Because life doesn't have to be so hard.* New York, NY: HarperCollins.

Cashman, K. (1999). *Leadership from the inside out.* Provo, UT: Executive Excellence.

Catalyst. (2004). *Advancing African American women in the workplace: What managers need to know.* New York, NY: Catalyst.

Couto, R. A. (1995). Defining a Citizen Leader. In J. Wren, *The Leader's Companion: Insights on Leadership Through the Ages* (pp. 11–17). New York, NY: The Free Press.

Cox, T. (1994). *Cultural diversity in organizations: Theory, research, and practice.* San Francisco, CA: Berrett-Koehler.

Cox, T., & Beale, R. L. (1997). *Developing competency to manage diversity: Readings, cases, and activities.* San Francisco, CA: Berrett-Koehler.

Csikszentmihalyi, M. (1996). *Creativity: Flow the psychology of discovery and invention.* New York, NY: HarperCollins.

Darlington, G. (1996). Culture: A theoretical review. In P. Joynt, & M. Warner (Eds.). *Managing across cultures: Issues and perspectives* (pp. 3–54). Boston, MA: International Thomson Business.

Derr, C. B., Roussillon, S., & Bournois, F. (Eds.). (2002). *Cross-cultural approaches to leadership development*. Westport, CT: Quorum.

Drucker, P. (1994, November). The age of social transformation. *The Atlantic Monthly*, 1–20.

Earley, P. C., & Mosakowski, E. (2004). Cultural intelligence. *Harvard Business Review, 82*(10), 139–146.

Earley, P. C, & Peterson, R. S. (2004). The elusive cultural chameleon: Cultural intelligence as a new approach to intercultural training for the global manager. *Academy of Management and Learning, 3*(1), 100–115.

Earley, P., Ang, S., & Tan, J-S. (2006). *CQ: Developing cultural intelligence at work*. Stanford, CA: Stanford University Press.

Fadiman, A. (1998). *The Spirit Catches You and You Fall Down*. Farrar, Straus and Giroux.

Flavell, J. (1979). Metacognition and cognitive monitoring: A new era of cognitive-development inquiry. *American Psychologist, 34*(10), pp. 906–911.

Frankl, V. (1984). *Man's search for meaning*. Boston, MA: Beacon Press.

Friedman, T. (2007). *The world is flat: A brief history of the twenty-first century*. New York, NY: Picador.

Gardner, H. (2004). *Changing minds: The art and science of changing our own and other people's minds*. Boston, MA: Harvard Business School Press.

Gardner, H. (2006). *Five minds for the future*. Cambridge, MA: Harvard Business School Press.

Gardner, H. E. (1983). *Frames of mind: The theory of multiple intelligences*. New York, NY: Basic Books.

Geertz, C. (1973). *The interpretation of cultures*. New York, NY: Basic Books.

Goldsmith, M. (2006). Leading new age professionals. In F. Hesselbein & M. Goldsmith (Eds.), *The leader of the future 2: Visions, strategies, and practices for the new era* (pp. 165–172). San Francisco, CA: Jossey-Bass.

Goldsmith, M., Greenberg, C. L., Robertson, A., & Hu-Chan, M. (2003). *Global leadership: The next generation*. Upper Saddle River, NJ: Financial Times Prentice Hall.

Goleman, D. (1995). *Emotional intelligence: Why it can matter more than IQ*. New York, NY: Bantam Books.

Goleman, D. (2006). *Social intelligence: The new science of human relationships*. New York, NY: Bantam Books.

Hall, E. T. (1981). *Beyond culture*. New York, NY: Random House.

Hall, E. T. (1990). *The silent language*. New York, NY: Anchor Books.

Heifetz, R. (1994). *Leadership without easy answers.* Boston, MA: Harvard University Press.

Hofstede, G. (1991). *Cultures and organizations: Software of the mind.* London, England: McGraw-Hill.

Hofstede, G. (2001). *Culture's consequences: Comparing values, behaviors, institutions, and organizations across nations.* Thousand Oaks, CA: Sage.

House, R. J., & Javidan, M. (2002). Overview of GLOBE. In R. J. House, P. J. Hanges, M. Javidan, P. W. Dorfman, & V. Gupta, *Culture, leadership, and organizations: The GLOBE study of 62 societies* (pp. 9–28). Thousand Oaks, CA: SAGE.

Hubbard, R. (2002). *Profitable promises: Essays on women, science, and health.* Monroe, ME: Common Courage Press.

Hurtado, A. (1996). Strategic suspensions: Feminists of color theorize the production of knowledge. In N. Goldberger, J. Tarule, B. Clinchy, & M. Belenky. (Eds.). *Knowledge, difference, and power: Essays inspired by women's ways of knowing* (pp. 372–392). New York, NY: HarperCollins.

Human resource management guide. (n.d.). Retrieved June 10, 2010, from http://www.hrmguide.com/diversity/job-market.htm

Janis, I. (1973, Autumn). Groupthink and group dynamics: A social psychological analysis of defective policy decisions. *Policy Studies Journal, 2*(1), pp. 19–25.

Katie, B. (2002). *Loving what is: Four questions that can change your life.* New York, NY: Three Rivers Press.

Kennedy, D. (2008). *Putting our differences to work: The fastest way to innovation, leadership, and high performance.* San Francisco, CA: Berrett-Koehler.

Koopman, P. L., Hartog, D. N., Konrad, E., et al. (1999). National culture and leadership profiles in Europe: Some results from the GLOBE study. *European Journal of Work and Organizational Psychology, 8*(4), 503–520.

Kotter, J. (1999). *What Leaders Really Do.* Boston, MA: Harvard Business Press.

Kouzes, J. M., & Posner, B. Z. (2002). *The leadership challenge.* San Francisco, CA: Jossey-Bass.

Lakoff, G. (2006, February 14). *Simple Framing.* Retrieved May 22, 2010, from Rockridge Institute, http://www.bswhn.org.au/Forum%20documents/Simple%20Framing.pdf

Langer, E. (1989). *Mindfulness.* New York, NY: Perseus Books.

Lawler, E. E., & Worley, C. (2006). *Built to Change: How to Achieve Sustained Organizational Effectiveness.* San Francisco, CA: Jossey-Bass.

LeBaron, M. (2003). Cross cultural communication. In G. Burgess, & H. Burgess, *Beyond Intractability.* Boulder, CO: Conflict Research Consortium, University of Colorado. Posted: July 2003 http://www.beyondintractability.org/essay/culture_negotiation/

Lein, M. (2004, Summer). Workforce opportunities in diversity: The melting pot. *Occupational Outlook Quarterly*, 28–37.

Lencioni, P. (2002). *The five dysfunctions of a team: A leadership fable.* San Francisco, CA: Jossey-Bass.

MacDonald, M. R. (2004). *Three minute tales: Stories from around the world to tell or read when time is short.* Little Rock, AR: August House Publishers.

Mead, G. H. (1925). The genesis of the self and social control. *International Journal of Ethics, 35*(3), 251–277.

Meharbian, A. (1971). *Silent Messages.* Belmond, CA: Wadsworth.

Mitchell, S. (1988). *Tao te ching.* New York, NY: Harper & Row.

Northouse, P. G. (2007). *Leadership: Theory and practice* (4th ed.). Thousand Oaks, CA: Sage.

Palmer, P. (1998). Leading from within. In L. C. Spears (Ed.), *Insights on leadership: Service, stewardship, spirit, and servant-leadership* (pp. 197–208). New York, NY: John Wiley & Sons.

Pink, D. H. (2006). *A Whole New Mind.* New York, NY: Riverhead Trade.

Purkey, W. (1988). An overview of self-concept theory for counselors. *ERIC Clearinghouse on Counseling and Personnel Services.* Ann Arbor, MI: ERIC/CAPS Digest ED304630.

Rogers, C. R. (1980). *A way of being.* New York, NY: Houghton Mifflin.

Rogers, E. M., & Steinfatt, T. M. (1999). *Intercultural communication.* Prospect Heights, IL: Waveland Press.

Salzberg, B. (2008, Nov./Dec.). Diversify or die: Why companies need to embrace diversity or risk being left behind. *DiversityInc.,* 122–123. Retrieved from http://www.diversityinc-digital.com/diversityincmedia/200811#pg124

Schein, E. H. (2006). *Organizational Culture and Leadership.* San Francisco, CA: Jossey-Bass.

Senge, P. M. (1990). *The fifth discipline: The art and practice of the learning organization.* New York, NY: Doubleday.

Sumedho, A. (2001). *Teachings of a Buddhist monk.* Totnes, United Kingdom: Buddhist Publishing Group.

Tavris, C., & Aronson, E. (2007). *Mistakes were made (but not by me): Why we justify foolish beliefs, bad decisions, and hurtful acts.* Orlando, FL: Harcourt.

Taylor, W. C. (1999, May 31). *The Leader of the Future.* Retrieved October 12, 2010, from Fast Company: http://www.fastcompany.com/magazine/25/heifetz.html

Thomas, D. C., & Inkson, K. (2003). *Cultural intelligence: People skills for global business.* San Francisco, CA: Berrett-Koehler Publishers.

Toossi, M. (2006). A new look at long-term labor force projections to 2050. *Monthly Labor Review, 129* (11), 19–39.

U.S. Census Bureau. (2004). *U.S. Interim Projections by Age, Sex, Race, and Hispanic Origin.* Retrieved May 23, 2010, from Population Projections Web site: http://www.census.gov/ipc/www/usinterimproj/

U.S. Census Bureau. (2009). Retrieved October 12, 2010, from Key Economic Indicator DatabaseWeb site: http://www.census.gov/econ/currentdata/ftd/?pr ogramCode=FTD&geoLevelCode=US&yearStart=2009&yearEnd=2009&c ategoryCode=BOPGS&dataTypeCode=EXP&adjusted=0&adjusted=1&not adjusted=0&errorData=0&submit=GET+DATA#report

Wheatley, M. J. (2006). *Leadership and the new science: Discovering order in a chaotic world.* San Francisco, CA: Berrett-Koehler.

Wheatley, M. J. (n.d.) *What does it mean to unlearn?* Retrieved June 11, 2010, from www.swaraj.org: http://www.swaraj.org/shikshantar/unlearning_margaret.htm

Whorf, B. L. (1956). *Language, thought, and reality: Selected writings of Benjamin Lee Whorf* (J. B. Carroll, Ed.). Boston, MA: MIT Press.

Yen, H. (2010, June 10). Minority population growing. Retrieved October 12, 2010, from Washington Times: http://www.washingtontimes.com/ news/2010/jun/10/minority-population-growing/

Index

Announcing the Business Expert Press Digital Library

Concise E-books Business Students Need for Classroom and Research

This book can also be purchased in an e-book collection by your library as

- a one-time purchase,
- that is owned forever,
- allows for simultaneous readers,
- has no restrictions on printing, and
- can be downloaded as PDFs from within the library community.

Our digital library collections are a great solution to beat the rising cost of textbooks. e-books can be loaded into their course management systems or onto student's e-book readers.

The BUSINESS EXPERT PRESS digital libraries are very affordable, with no obligation to buy in future years.

For more information, please visit WWW.BUSINESSEXPERT.COM/LIBRARIES. To set up a trial in the United States, please contact SHERI ALLEN at *sheri.allen@globalepress.com*; for all other regions, contact NICOLE LEE at **NICOLE.LEE@IGROUPNET.COM**.

OTHER TITLES IN OUR HUMAN RESOURCE MANAGEMENT AND ORGANIZATIONAL BEHAVIOR COLLECTION
Series Editors: Jean Phillips and Stan Gully

Dynamic Strategies for Small Businesses

Process Mapping and Management

Achieving Excellence in Management: Identifying and Learning from Bad Practices

Succeeding at the Top: A Self-Paced Workbook for Newly Appointed CEOs and Executives

Operational Leadership

Strategic Planning: Fundamentals for Small Business

Strategic Analysis: A Structured Approach

Grow by Focusing on What Matters: Competitive Strategy in 3-Circles